ROBERTO FILIPPETTI

THE GREAT EVENT ACCORDING TO GIOTTO

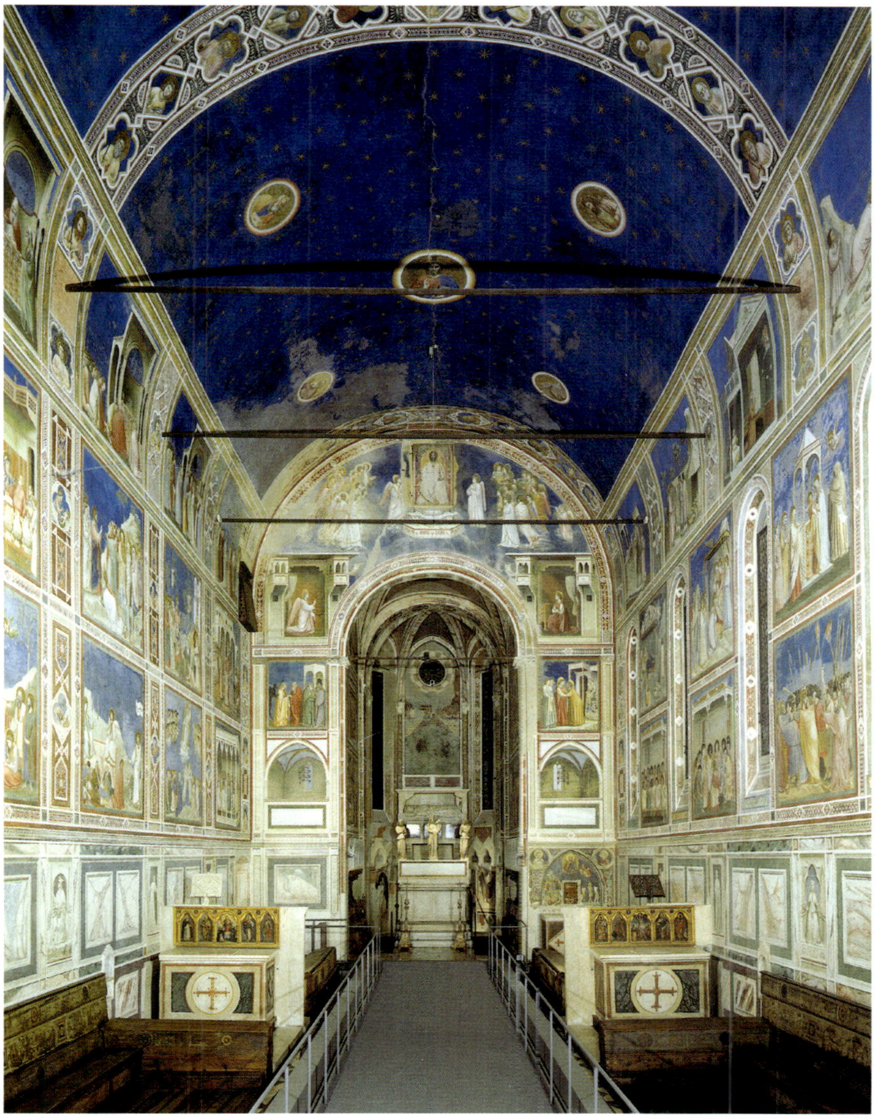

ITACA

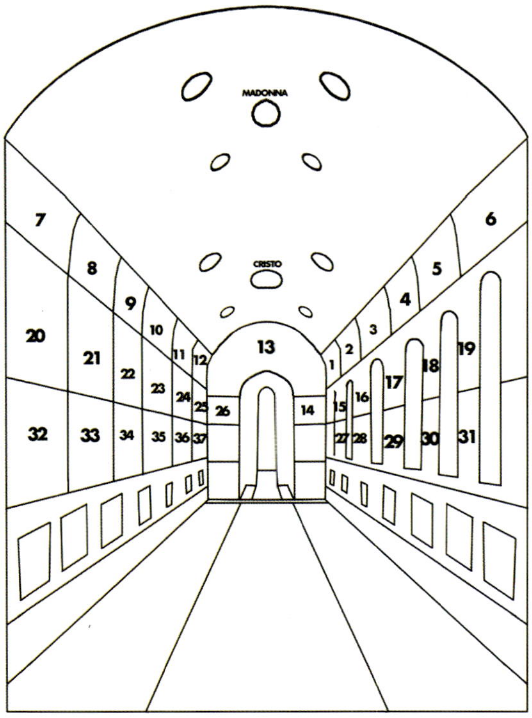

Testo
© Roberto Filippetti
E-mail: robertofilippetti@libero.it

Translated by
Janet Sethre

Stampa
OGM - Padova

Edizione
ITACA
Via Provinciale Lughese, 1880
48014 Castel Bolognese (RA)
Tel. 0546 656188 Fax 0546 652098
E-mail: itaca@itacalibri.it
www.itacalibri.it

su licenza
© Giorgio Deganello Editore
Via SS. Martino e Solferino, 41/A
35122 PADOVA
Tel. 049 660888 - Fax 049 666101
E-mail: giorgio.deganello@tin.it

ISBN 88-87022-73-9
First edition after
the April 2002 restauration

Finito di stampare
nel mese di aprile 2002

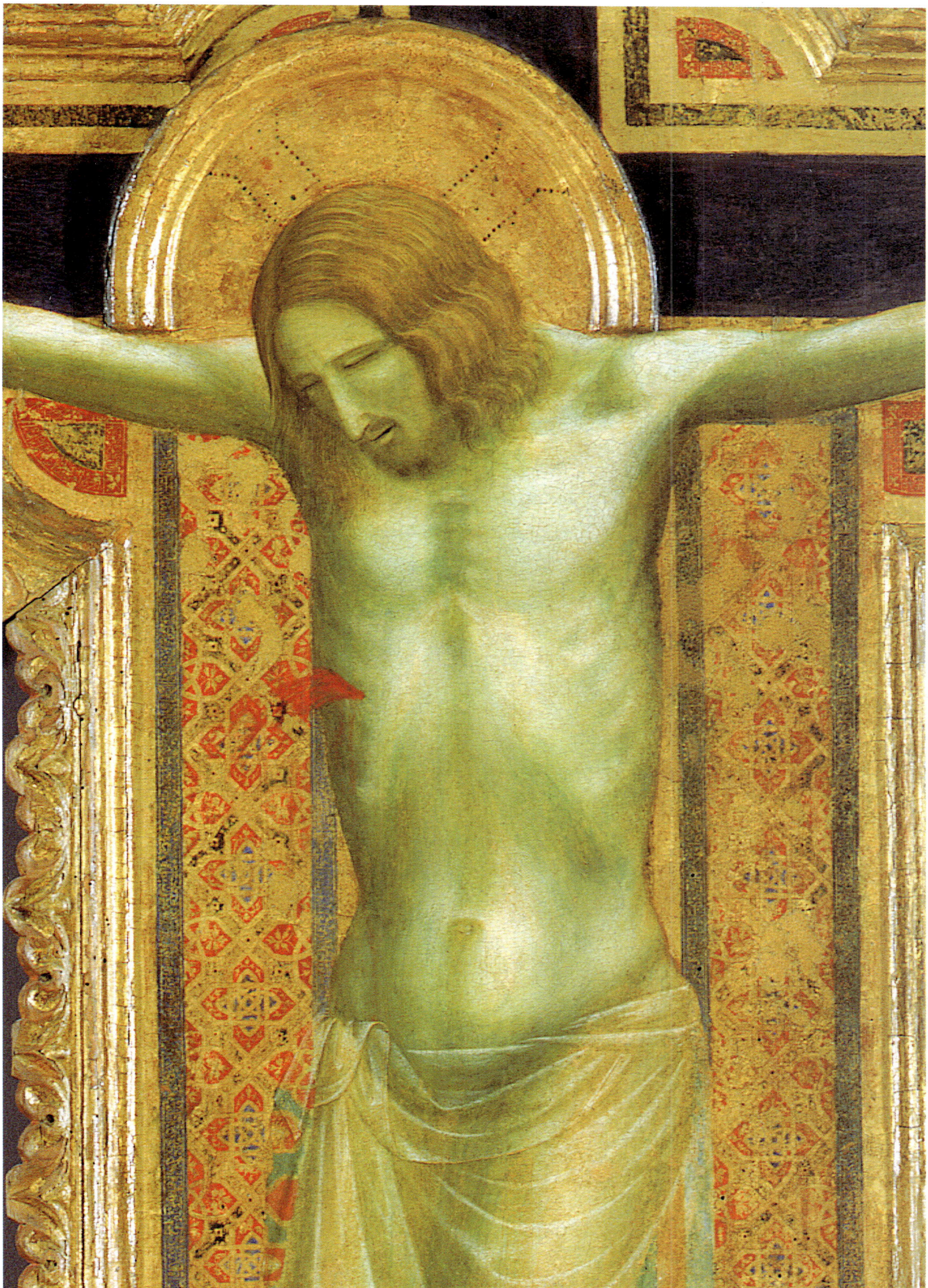

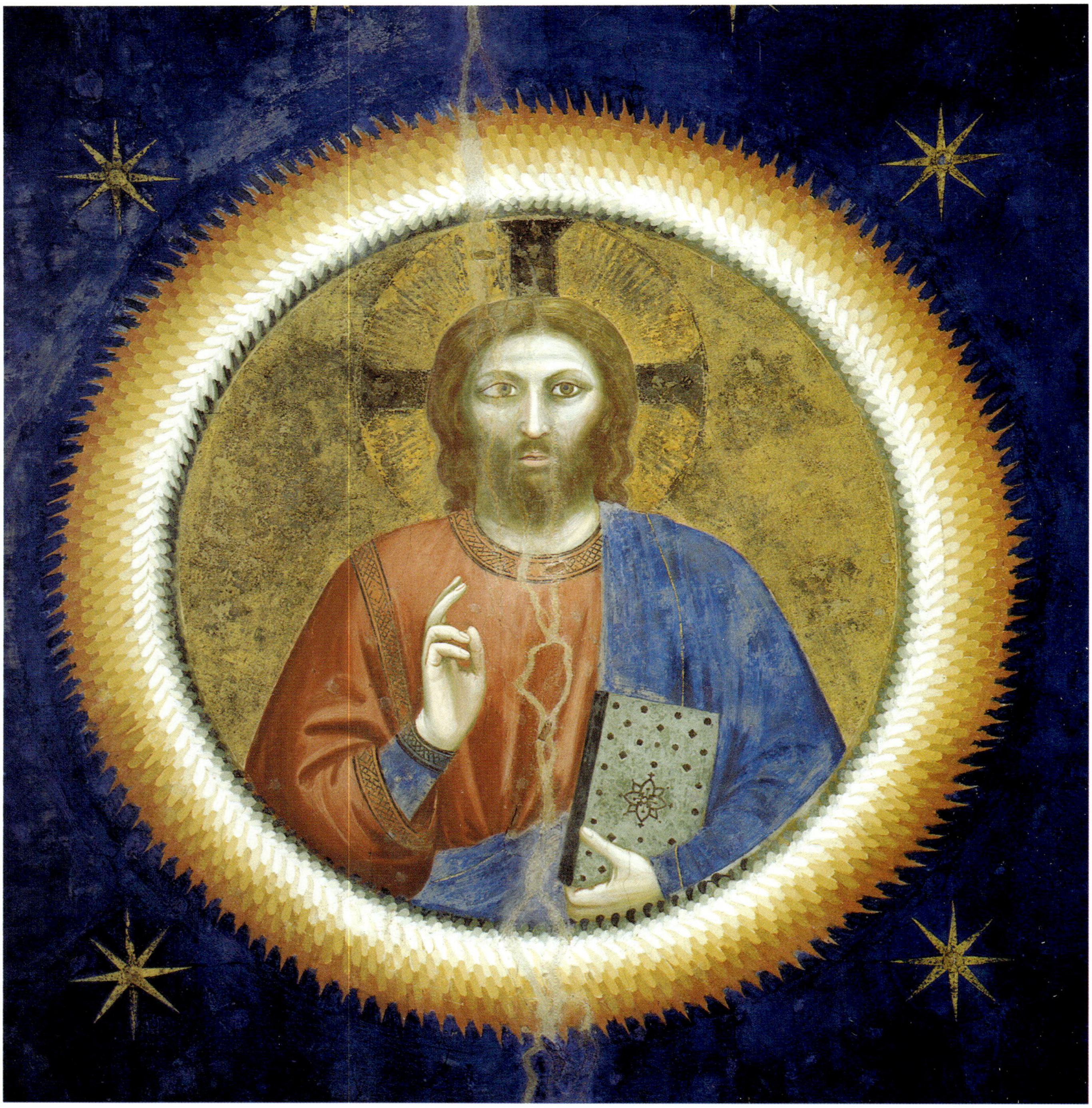

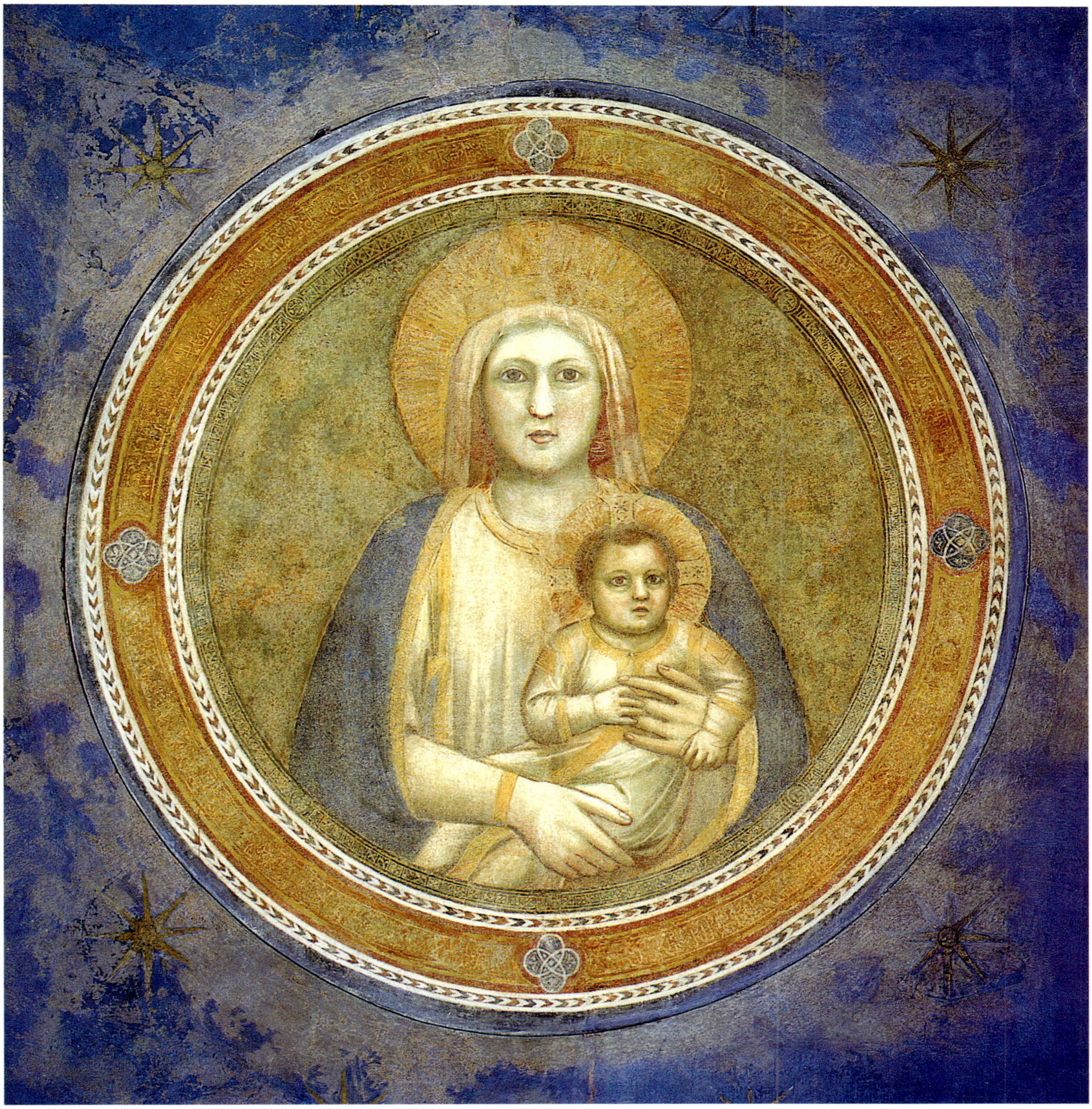

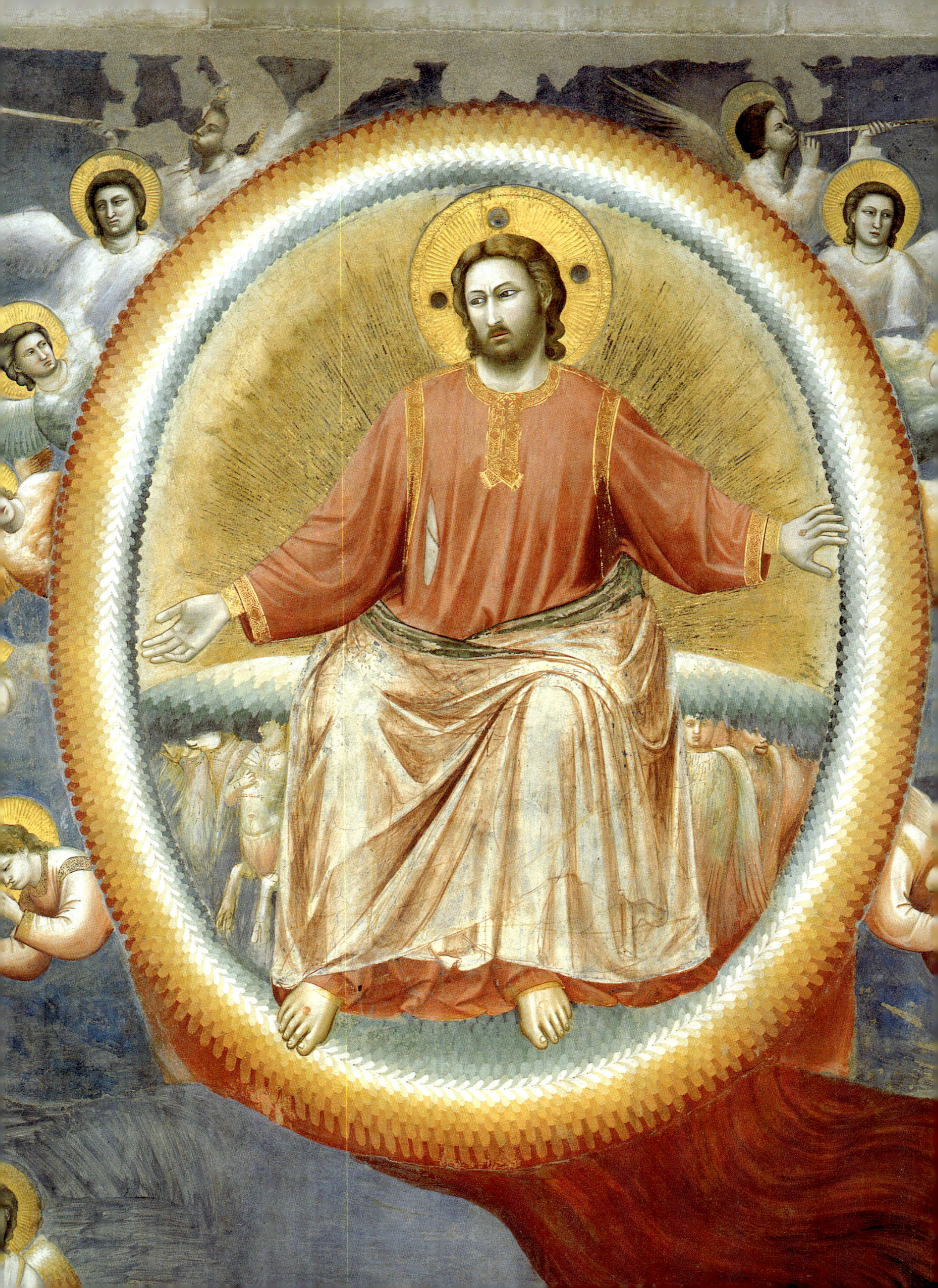

THE GREAT EVENT ACCORDING TO GIOTTO

At the Arena of Padua, in the Scrovegni chapel, Giotto dramatized the Event: the one which Christendom celebrated in the Jubilee of 1300.

He had worked in Rome itself on that occasion, and was well acquainted with the mausoleum of Galla Placidia in Ravenna, which inspired him, once he had reached Padua around the year 1303, as he began to paint his greatest masterpiece. The Scrovegni Chapel is a very simple building, on the outside, with its bricks solidly resting on the bare ground. However, once one has crossed the threshold, a piece of world opens out which is not of this world: for Beauty — as the Jubilees of 1300 and 2000 attes — entered this world and was revealed to the wonderstruck gaze of those whose heart remains childlike. Etymologically, the word "monument" means a "sign that makes us remember". But the meanings of this Chapel, which were clear for so many centuries, today appear enigmatic to many. They seem incapable of reminding us of anything; they seem to be expressed in an unknown language.

Often, scholarly studies tend to complicate things, rather than simplify them. Our aim here is simply to let this monument speak, and to listen to its message: to what "Giotto really meant to say" (Claudio Bellinati); since "Beauty is the splendor of Truth", we are keen to grasp the iconic poetry of vertical and frontal correspondences; the symbolism of colors, numbers, architectural perspectives. Alongside Dante, Giotto stands at the apex of a "culture in which all details, excluding none, are involved as in a single note or a single song, without any disharmony" (L. Giussani). One who has had the fortune to visit the chapel hundreds of times, with numerous groups of friends, has each time been spurred to grasp a new, surprising detail, within the grand symphony: details often seized on by the curious eye of a schoolboy, and then confirmed later on in the pages of some weighty scholarly essay.

The day of the first dedication of the Scrovegni Chapel was March 25, 1303; the second dedication, to "Holy Mary of Charity at the Arena", occurred when the frescoes had been completed, on March 25, 1305, the Feast of the Annunciation. Mary of the Annunciation, or "of Charity": for charity is not any generous effort of mine to do good (which ends up, sooner or later, by tiring me out), but the initiative of God who became flesh on March 25 of the year Zero, by way of the archangel Gabriel who brought the annunciation to Mary. *Gratis*, in Latin, *charis*, in Greek: gratuitousness, charity, the absolutely gratuitous gift of God to man, by way of the womb (and the freedom to consent) of a young girl aged sixteen or seventeen years.

To the left and right of the great triumphal arch stand the angel and Mary, while at the top, in a rectangular painting, we seen the throne of God toward which Gabriel is ascending. This is the Alpha of redeeming charity, the prologue in heaven of the redeeming Event. During the Middle Ages, March 25, the Feast of the Annunciation, was New Year's day, both in Padua and Florence: the beginning of a new time cycle, at the moment when we remember the Eternal which has entered time.

Once we have crossed the threshold, a symbol of faith in Christ — the gate of the fold — after climbing up three steps, a single space opens our before us, a single nave, though divided into three parts. The nave is cut by the iconostasis, once presided over by Giotto's Crucifix: this is Christ, gateway to the father's mercy. Finally, we come to the presbytery and the apse, with a round window from which sunlight pours forth at dawn: here is Christ risen, the sure gateway to hope, which each day rises, illuminates, warms and "orients" life There are three apses as well: beside the true one are two small painted apses, in fine perspective. In the triumphal arch an ideal triangle unites the throne of God the Father to the angel Gabriel, on the left, and the Lady of the Annunciation, on the right. On the back wall, Christ the Judge has just descended from the throne, which appears in the form of a three-mullioned window: a single, bright window, it is divided into three parts. In the starry heaven of the vault (crossed by ornamental stripes at the beginning, in the middle and at the end) shines the sun of Christ the Almighty, his hand raised in blessing. Three of its fingers are united: the thumb, ring finger and little finger; while the index finger and middle finger are crossed to indicate (in opposition to the Catharist heresy, forefather to today's New Age spiritualism) that in the person of Christ, the divine nature and the human one are inseparable. In short, Giotto continually speaks to us of the "Unity and Trinity of God", as he narrates the other main Mystery: the Incarnation, Passion, Death and Resurrection of our Lord Jesus Christ.

We may follow many other threesomes in the frescoes. The temple tabernacle appears three times: in the driving out of Joachim, the presentation of Mary, and the presentation of Jesus. The gates of Jerusalem appear three times. Three times can we note the rending of robes: in the angel at the foot of the cross, the high priest, and the vice of wrath. Three times do we see the Christ-bearing donkey, "cristò-foros": in the Nativity, the flight to Egypt, and the palm scene. Three "photograms" contained in the same architectural frame narrate the sequence of the Virgin's marriage. The last supper appears three times. Three times do we meet Magdalene at Christ's feet: in the *Crucifixion, Mourning over the dead Christ*, and *Resurrection* ...

The first gesture made, almost instinctively, by anyone crossing the threshold to the main entrance, is to raise the eyes, drawn magnetically by the blue sky: first of all, Giotto tears us from our distraction and brings us back into our selves, reminding us that God has created in us a hungering, thirsting heart. This is called "de-sire": the thirst for stars, a yearning for the heaven of felicity (the Middle Ages has handed down to us our passion for etymologies, which often conceal, as we shall see, the "key" to the frescoes). Grygiel would call it "an-echesis": a cry echoing upwards. If we are devoid of this wishful, yearning curiosity, the initiative of God who descends from heaven ("cat-echesis": the singing of the sweet News —"ev-angelos"— which echoes downward) suddenly slips by without leaving a trace. Let us contemplate, then, this precious lapis lazuli blue, which is deflected from the vault onto each and every one of Giotto's frescoes. It symbolizes the heaven of the good Mystery, for all reality dwells beneath the heavenly embrace of the merciful Father. Let us contemplate it wherever it has been preserved, and let us imagine it in places where the precious blue tint, applied with a binding agent onto the dry plaster to avoid being damaged by a wet "a fresco" lime surface, has fallen away.

We note such spots in the capes of Jesus and Mary.
Against a golden background, in the blue vault of heaven, stand out Christ-the-sun and Our Lady-the-moon, extraordinarily large heavenly bodies surrounded by the eight prophet-planets and by a myriad of little stars (more than seven hundred, symbolizing the saints). Having thus come back to our selves — conscious of being "de-siring" creatures — we look around. And we see that we have reached home (the Italian word for cathedral, "duomo", comes from "domo", Latin for home). We are in a fine, well-proportioned house. Its measurements are those of the temple of Salomon: 21.50 by 8.50 by 12.80 (see Kings 6 sqq.). Here, everything assists the memory: for here we move among the pages of an illumined manuscript — the *Biblia pauperum* —in which we are only asked to stand with our eyes wide open. Much observation is asked of us, and little intellectualistic fanciness. Then we move, led by a nave (meaning also "ship"), whose pilot takes us into port; or we walk securely down a road oriented toward the good Destiny (East), while from the southern windows flow light and warmth. Instead, on the northern wall there are no windows: against the cold and darkness of Evil we must struggle, raising an uncrossable sea barrier.
Home, ship, road, and above all, painted Bible: Giotto has "staged" the Jubilee *Event* of the Incarnation: fifty years of history, from the Immaculate Conception of Mary, around 17 BC, through the Nativity, up to the completion of the Redemption in the year 33 AD—in three splendid "registers". A true Event, occurring at a precise moment in the past; a Fact that reaches us with its splendor and, in the present, makes us love goodness and feel disgust for evil: here are the *Virtues* and *Vices*, in the fourth, monochrome "register". This event will reach completion when the judging mercy of Christ returns, at the end of time: note the *Final Judgment* on the contra-façade.
The Event, according to Giotto.

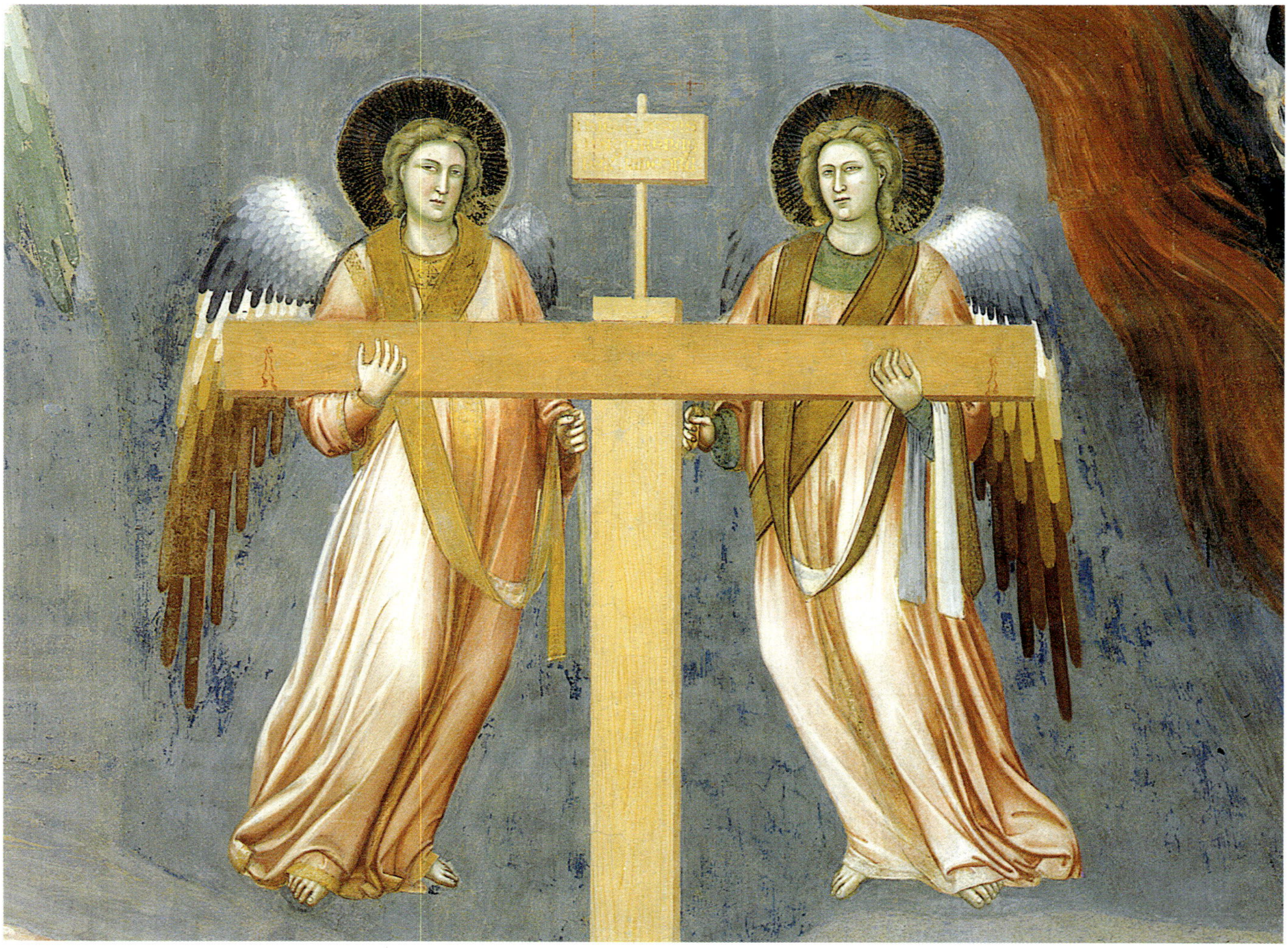

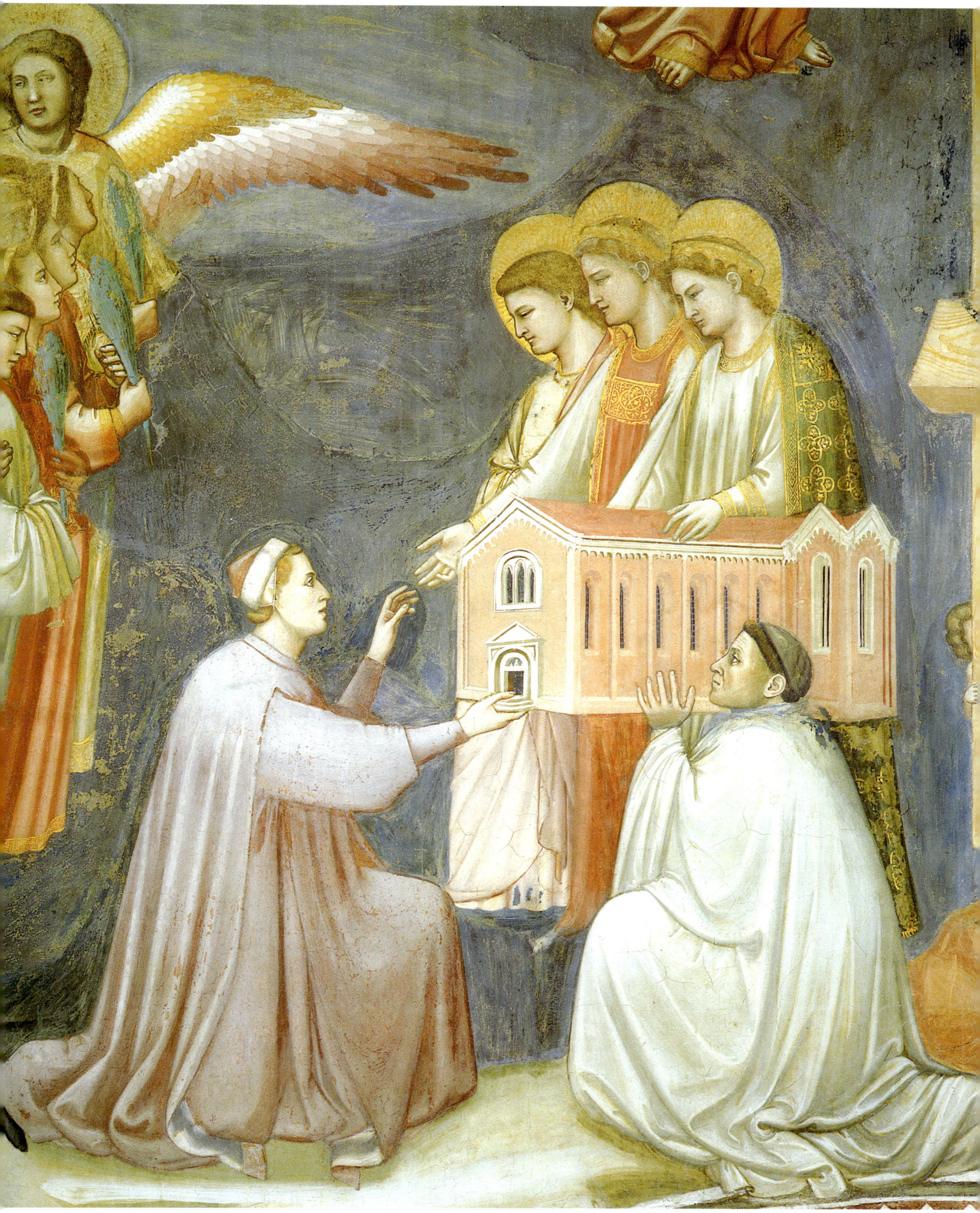

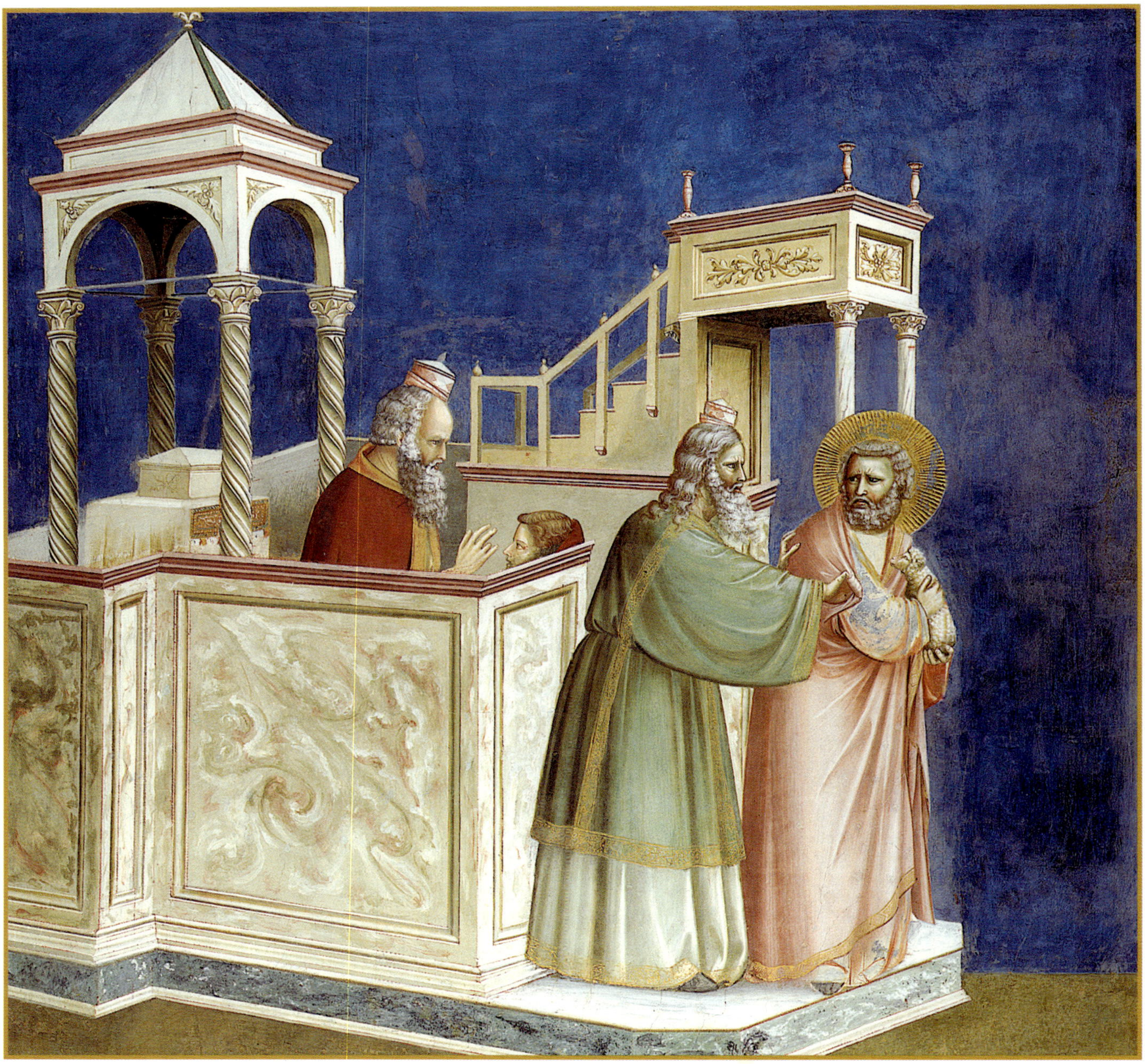

1. Joachim driven from the temple

In the high area above the windows, on the south wall, we find six frescoes referring to the Feast of December 8: the Immaculate Conception of Mary. In the first, Joachim — who will be Jesus' maternal grandfather — is violently shoved around by Ruben the scribe, and driven out of the temple, since he is sterile: a condition considered dishonorable by the Jews. His eyes express great pain; in his arms he hugs the sacrificial kid which has been refused by the priests (they are dressed in red and green, like the high priests who will condemn Jesus fifty years later).
Within the temple walls rises a tabernacle, supported by twisting columns: this is the "sancta sanctorum" containing the Ark of the Covenant; but it resembles the ciborium fashioned by Arnolfo di Cambio which sits on an altar in the Roman Church of Santa Cecilia in Trastevere. In the lower area stands the table/altar of the *Last supper*.

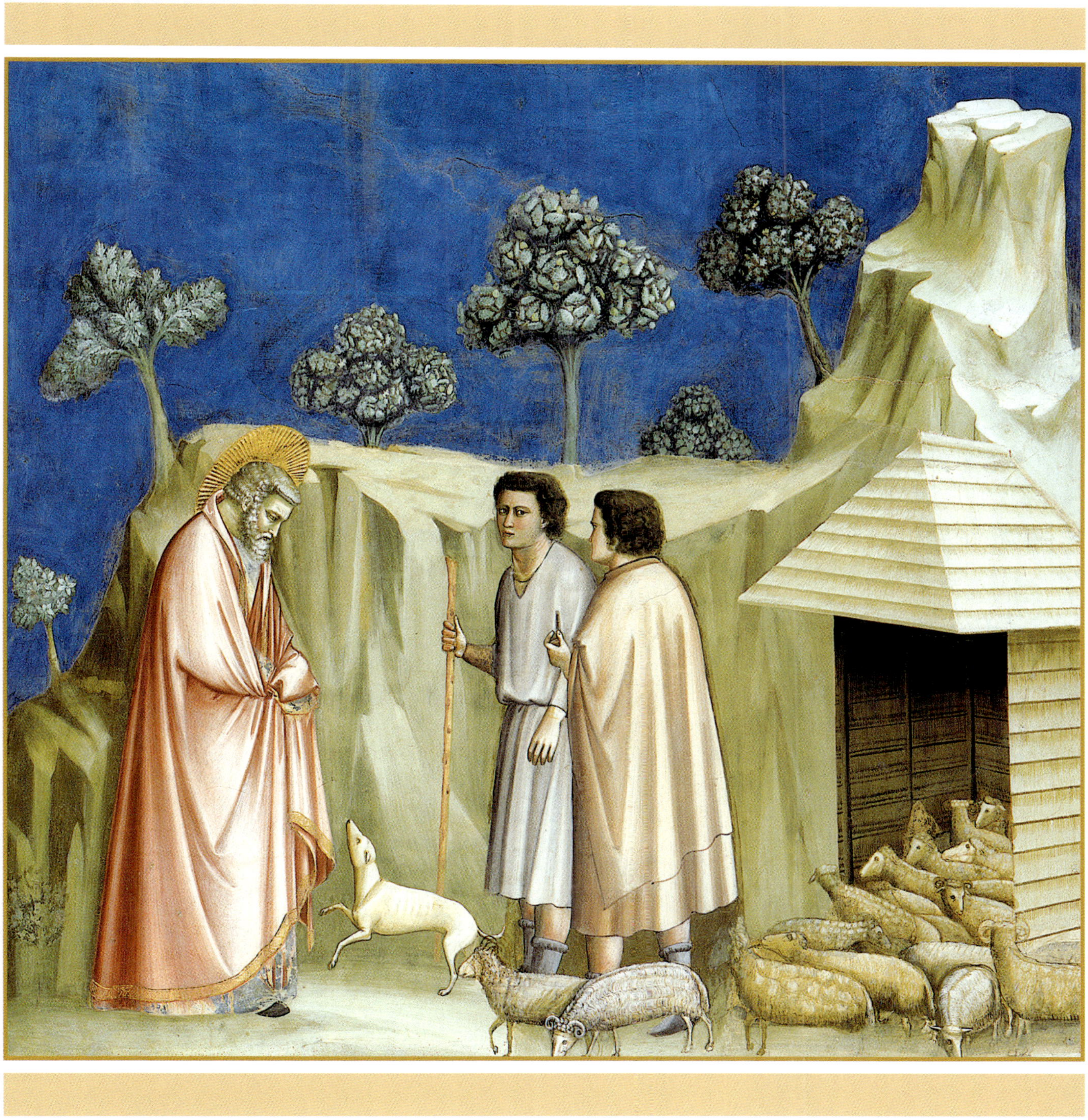

2. Joachim among the shepherds
In suffering, Joachim goes to stay for five months "among his shepherds in the mountains", as we read in the apocryphal gospel of Pseudo-Matthew (PM): the two young men silently question one another, the plants are green, a little dog greets him joyously, but his heart is hardened, like the rocks framing the scene.

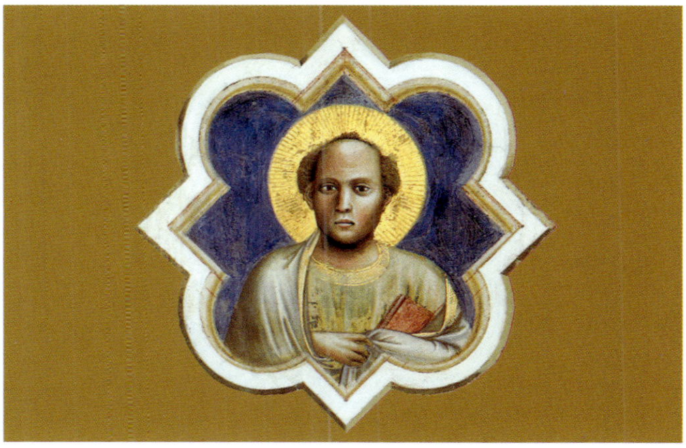

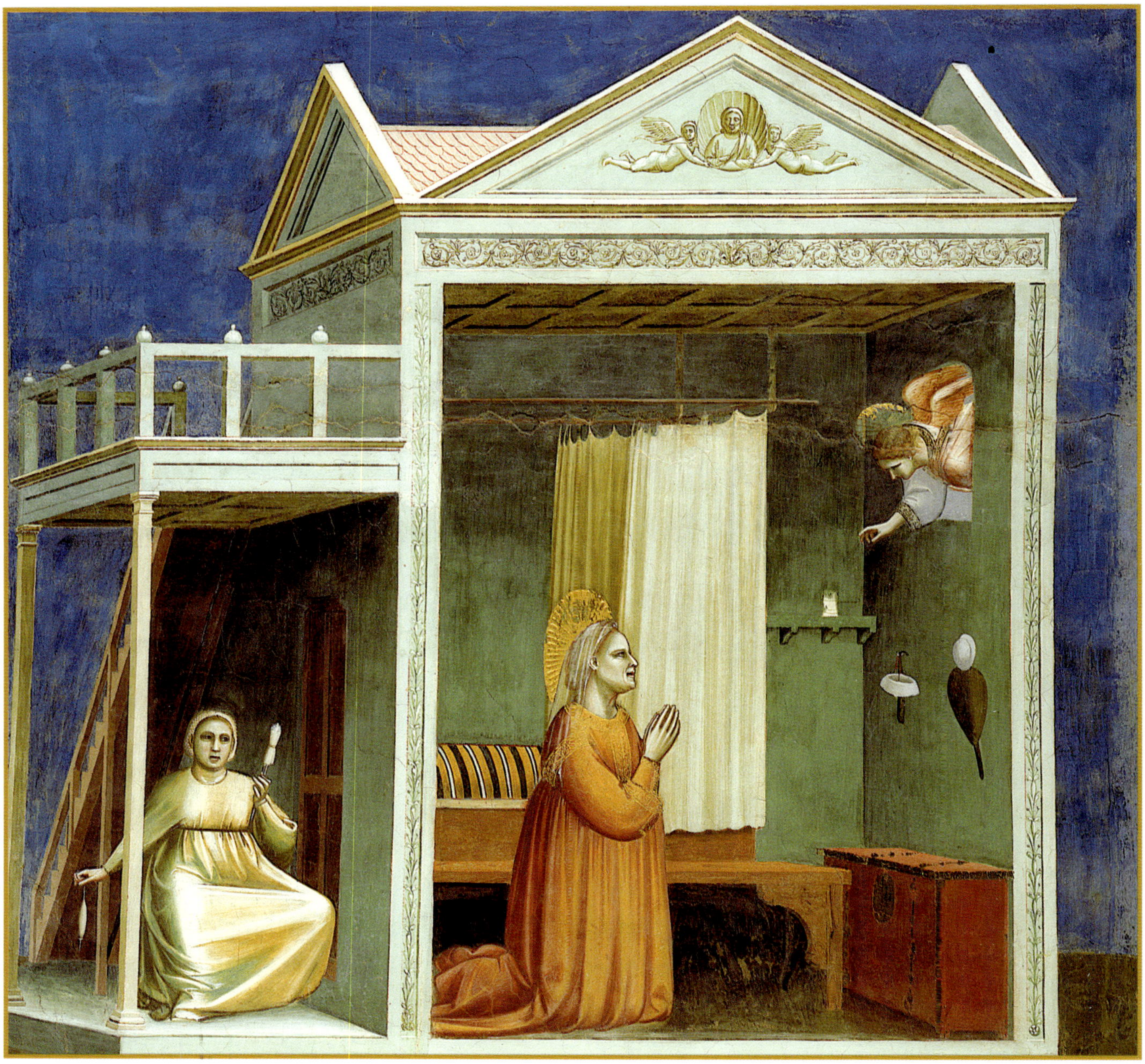

3. Annunciation to Anna

A fine house, with a porch and outer stairway. On the gable two angels hold up a seashell showing an image of Isaiah, the prophet of Mary. Here is the house where Joachim has not dared to return: outside, Judith the maid is spinning, while inside the event occurs: the archangel Gabriel appears at the window and brings to the elderly Anna the announcement that she will give birth to a daughter, Mary, "who will be admired forever" (PM). The radiant apparition makes Anna's face and the bed curtain glow.

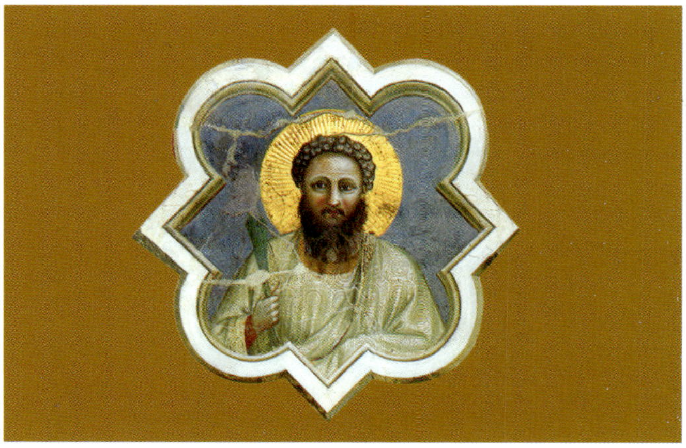

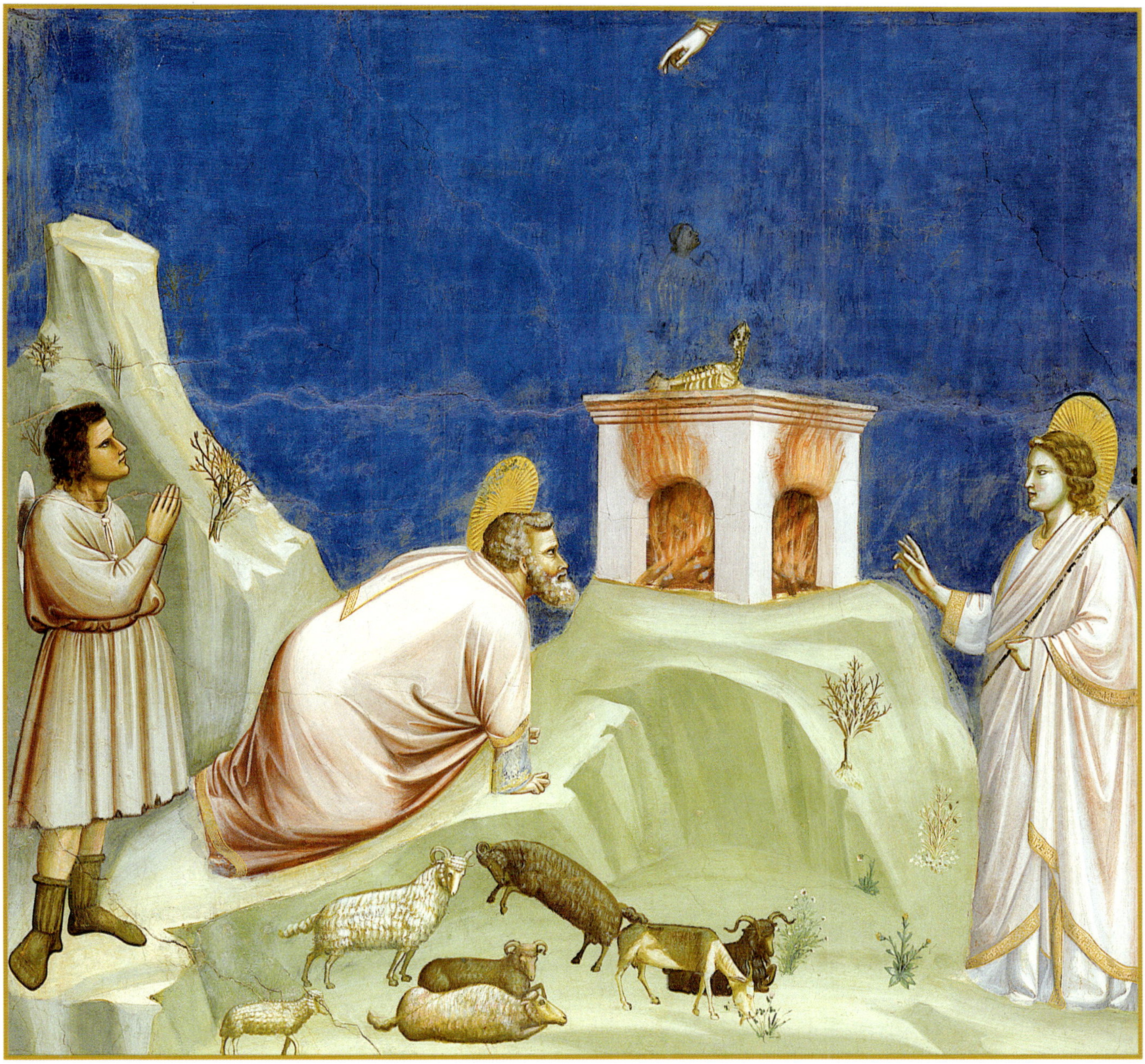

4. Joachim's sacrifice
Joachim has passed from affliction to the state of beggar, in a landscape which is specular to the preceding one: is lies prone, his chin brushing the ground, before the sacrificial victim burning on the altar. There is a triangle of hands: those of the shepherd and the angel point upwards, the Eternal Father's hand (whose face we do not see, for "whoever sees God dies") seems to bend downwards to accept the smoke of the holocaust. Between the sacrificed kid and the *manus Dei* is an angel, nearly invisible.

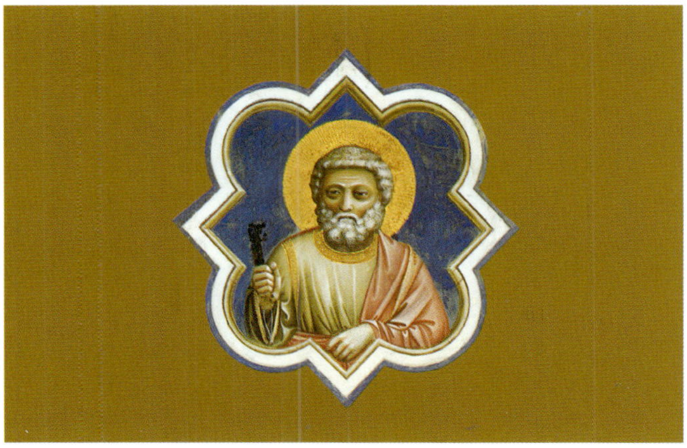

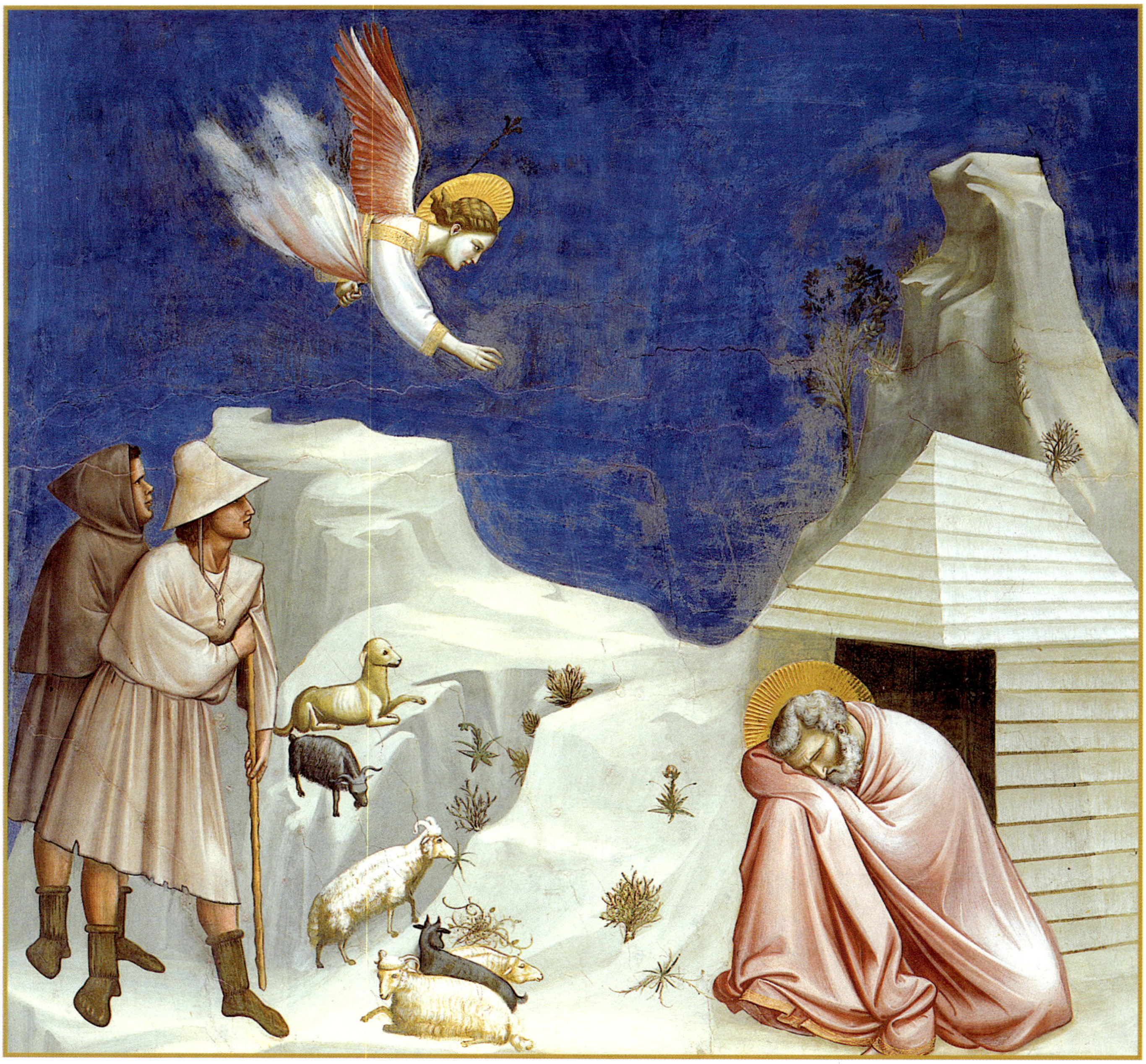

5. Joachim's dream

The shepherds keep watch in astonished silence. The little dog rests, in the evening twilight. Asleep before the fold (the same one appearing in the third-to-the-last picture), Joachim is visited in his dreams by his guardian angel, announcing that Anna, the sterile woman, will give birth to Mary: God has granted her prayer.

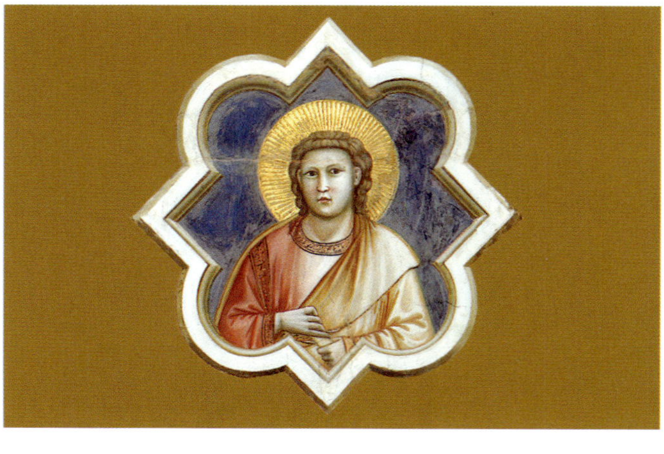

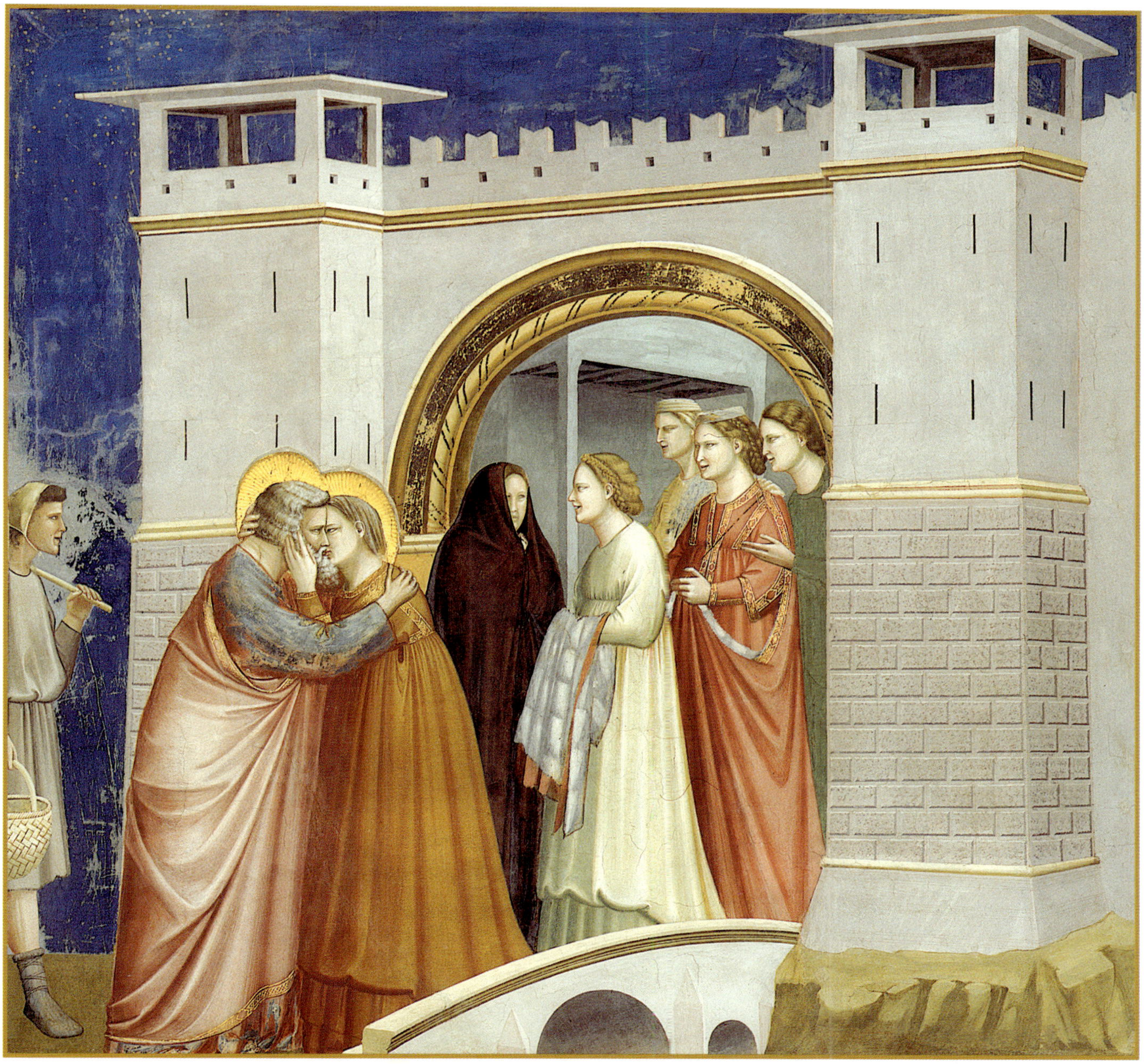

6. Joachim and Anna at the Golden Gate

Joachim and Anna embrace with new tenderness on the bridge, leading to the Golden Gate of Jerusalem (which resembles the arch of Augustus in Rimini). Their expression reveals a love which is deeply moved, mature, grateful.

Underneath the golden arch, on the left, is a woman dressed in black, her face half-veiled; her cold glance is directed elsewhere: while all the others, joyful and enchanted, converge on that embrace in which heaven and earth touch (this is the threshold of the Immaculate conception of Mary!), she di-verges. Symbolically, this is the Synagogue in the presence of the Church: the Old before the New Testament, night in the face of day. According to Bellinati, instead, "she is not the synagogue, but a widow in traditional dress, effectively revealing the profound contrast between the past widowhood of Anna and her refound happiness for her husband's return". But why not meld — as Dante might have done — the two interpretations, allegorical and literal?

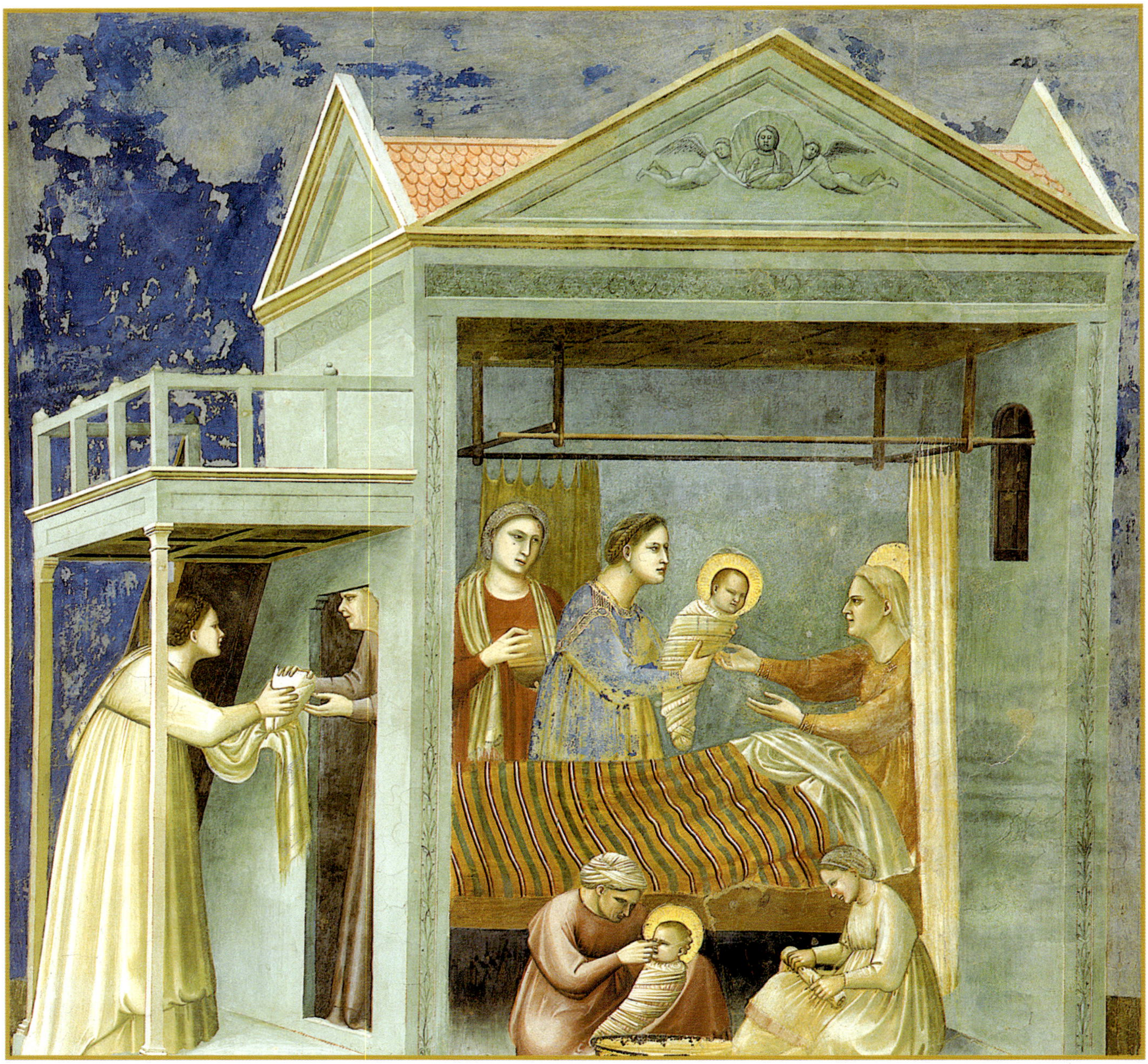

7. Nativity of Mary

Nine months have passed since the Immaculate Conception of Mary: the Virgin has been born, on September 8. We are in Anna's house: the same in which the Sterile Woman had been visited by the angel. The closed door of entry to the house, outside which a woman had sat spinning, is now open: it shelters an intense "conversation" of eye, hand, mute words. Instead, the window is closed through which the radiant angel of annunciation had entered: now it is the light of the three-mullioned window — the trinitary throne — which reaches the child, radiating outward from her.
Inside the room are two scenes: in the lower part, the newborn baby, who has just been swaddled, has her nose squeezed by one of Anna's friends (the same four friends appearing in the Golden Gate picture): that is "so that she will grow up pretty, according to popular tradition in many regions, including the Veneto" (Bellinati). Only at this point, in the upper part, is the child presented to her mother Anna, who stretches out her arms to embrace her. All the faces express a quiet joy.

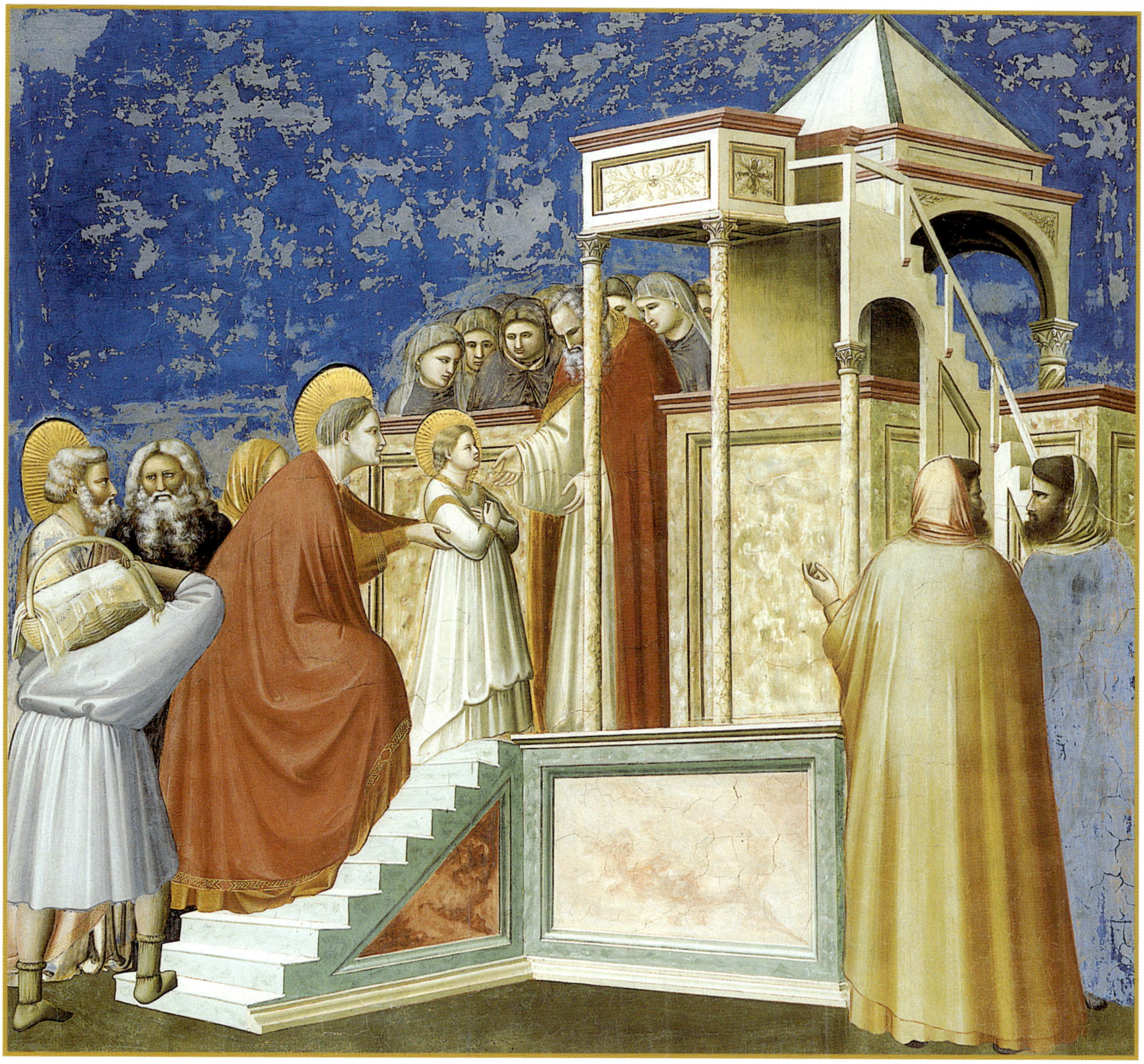

8. Presentation of Mary at the temple

Mary, a three-year-old child, is accompanied by her mother and presented at the temple. She stands on the uppermost of ten stairs (the Decalogue, the ancient law, now touching on the new). The temple is the same as in Joachim driven from the temple (though seen in specular opposition: a conversion of direction, non only of architectural structure!); and the priests are the same; however, the person who had descended mortified from the temple steps now watches in gratitude and wonderment as Anna and Mary ascend. Beside him stand Simeon, already very old, and Anna, the prophetess.

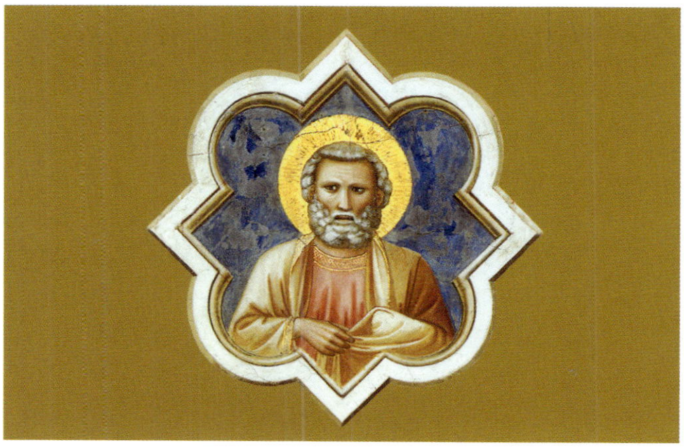

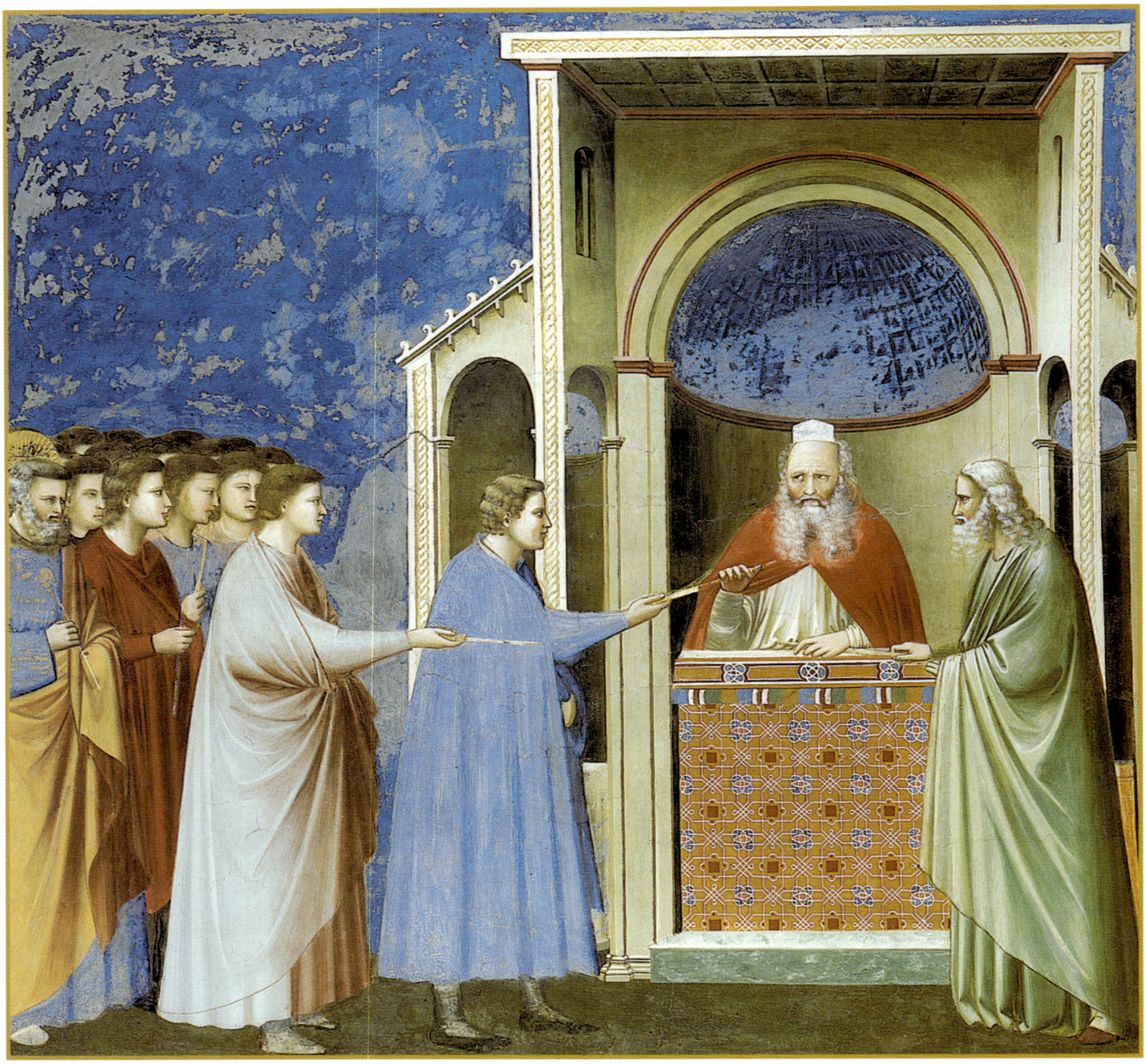

9. Consignment of the twigs

This is the first of three pictures framed by the same architectural background, similar to three photograms of some modern cinema sequence. Outside, the ephemeral, transitory blue of sky, which soon gives way to darkness; inside, in the bowl of the apse shows the blue of the eternal Mystery which is about to enter Time.

Giotto sets on stage the marriage of the Virgin. In the temple, which is formed like a three-nave church, the priest begins to lay on the altar the dry branches brought by the unmarried youths of the tribe of Judah, chosen by lot to safeguard the adolescent Mary "who has decided to consecrate herself to the Lord forever" (PM). The one who sees his twig flower will be chosen: the holder of the twig from which a dove takes flight.

Joseph appears: he is the last in line, the most mature. His face is identical to Joachim's: both are figures of paternity, as custodians of something not their own. The facial "type" of Joachim, and then of Joseph, will later be assumed by Peter, the Church's first Holy Father.

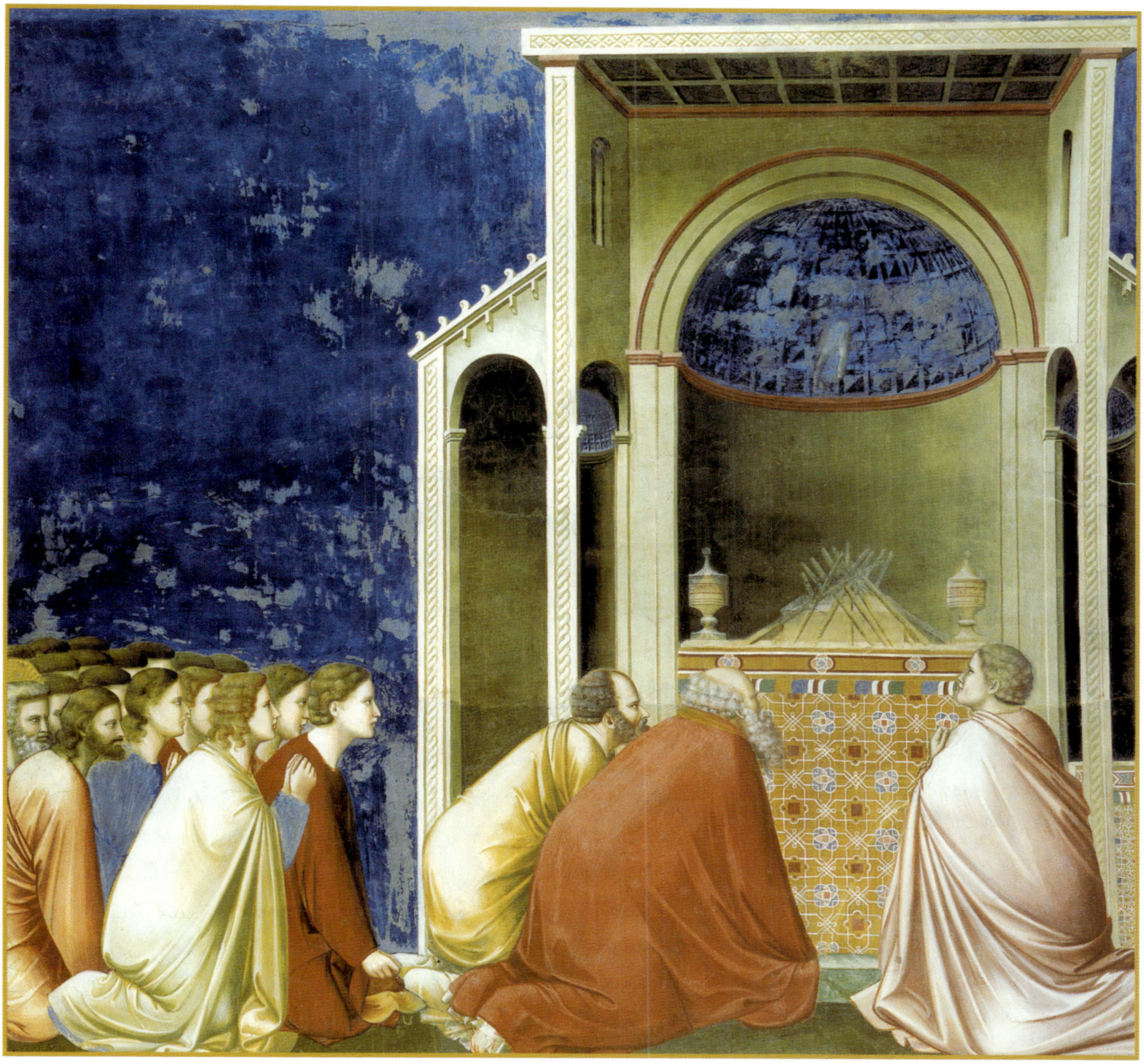

10. Prayer for the flowering of the twigs
Everyone is kneeling in prayer, anxiously awaiting the miraculous flowering. All kneel in adoration, symbolized by the two thuribles on the altar. The intensity of the men's gaze is striking. Joseph is still in last place, set aside, bearer of a "very small twig": so small that the priest "had hardly considered it" (PM).

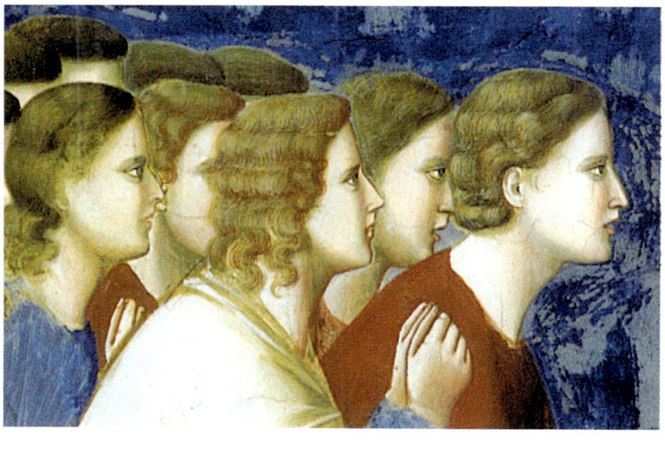

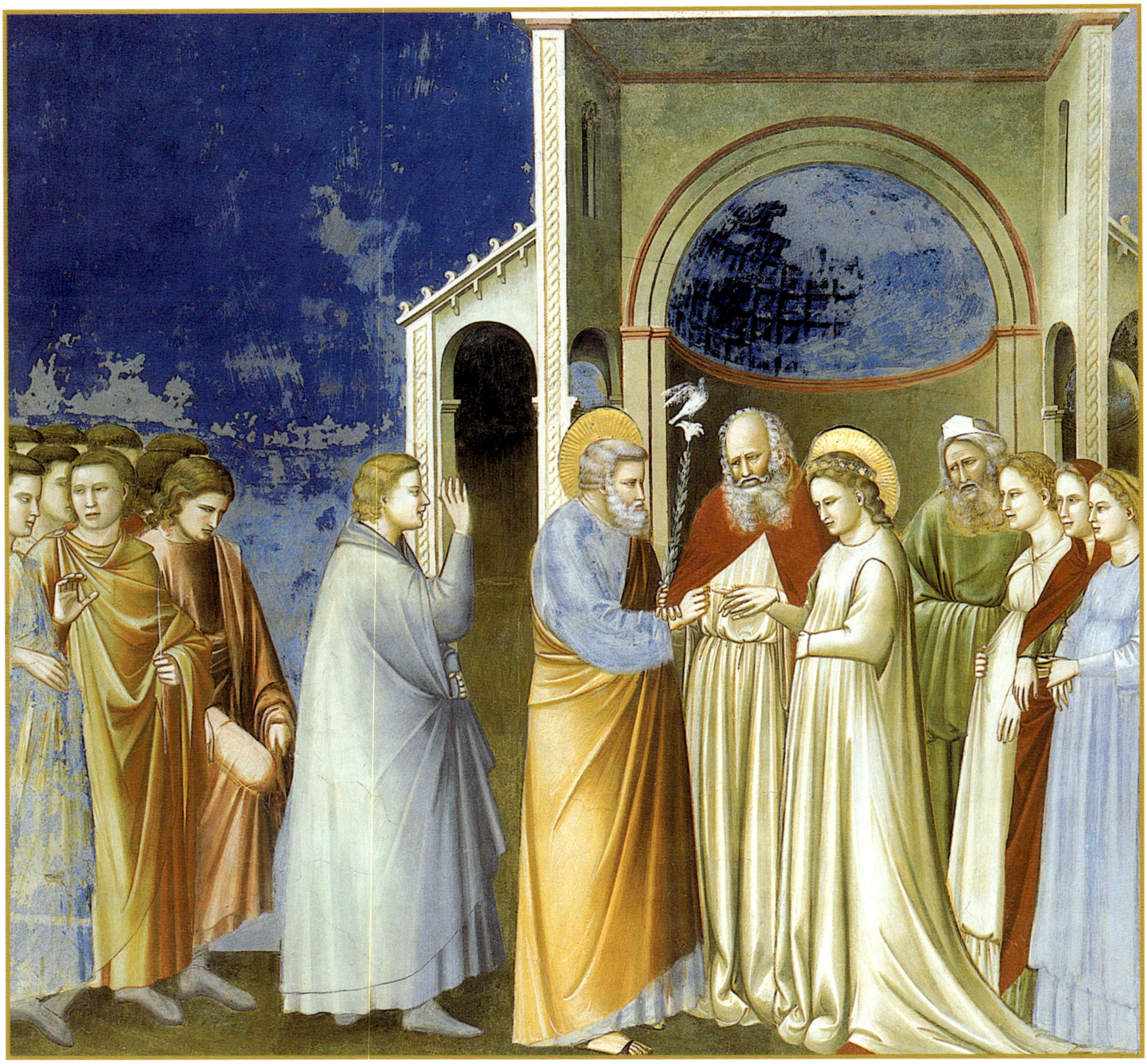

11. The wedding of Mary and Joseph

The last shall be the first. While outside, the group of the disappointed is led by a youth who breaks his twig over his knee, Joseph holds his rod, from which a lily has blossomed: the symbol of virginal marriage. The dove of the Holy Spirit is about to take flight from it, by whose works Mary will conceive Jesus. The priest joins Joseph and Mary in matrimony. In the very center of the apse cornice, she seems to be embraced by the architecture, and by the calm figures, in strong contrast to the compact group of disappointed youths remaining outside.

Here is a symphony of hands: those of the priest unite the right hand of bride and bridegroom; the witness' hand is raised. Here, above all, is a symphony of glances. Joseph gazes intently at Mary, full of "re-spect", of "re-guard" (looking again, looking in a new way: out of the corner of his eye he sees the Mystery reverberating in her). Humbly, Mary looks downward.

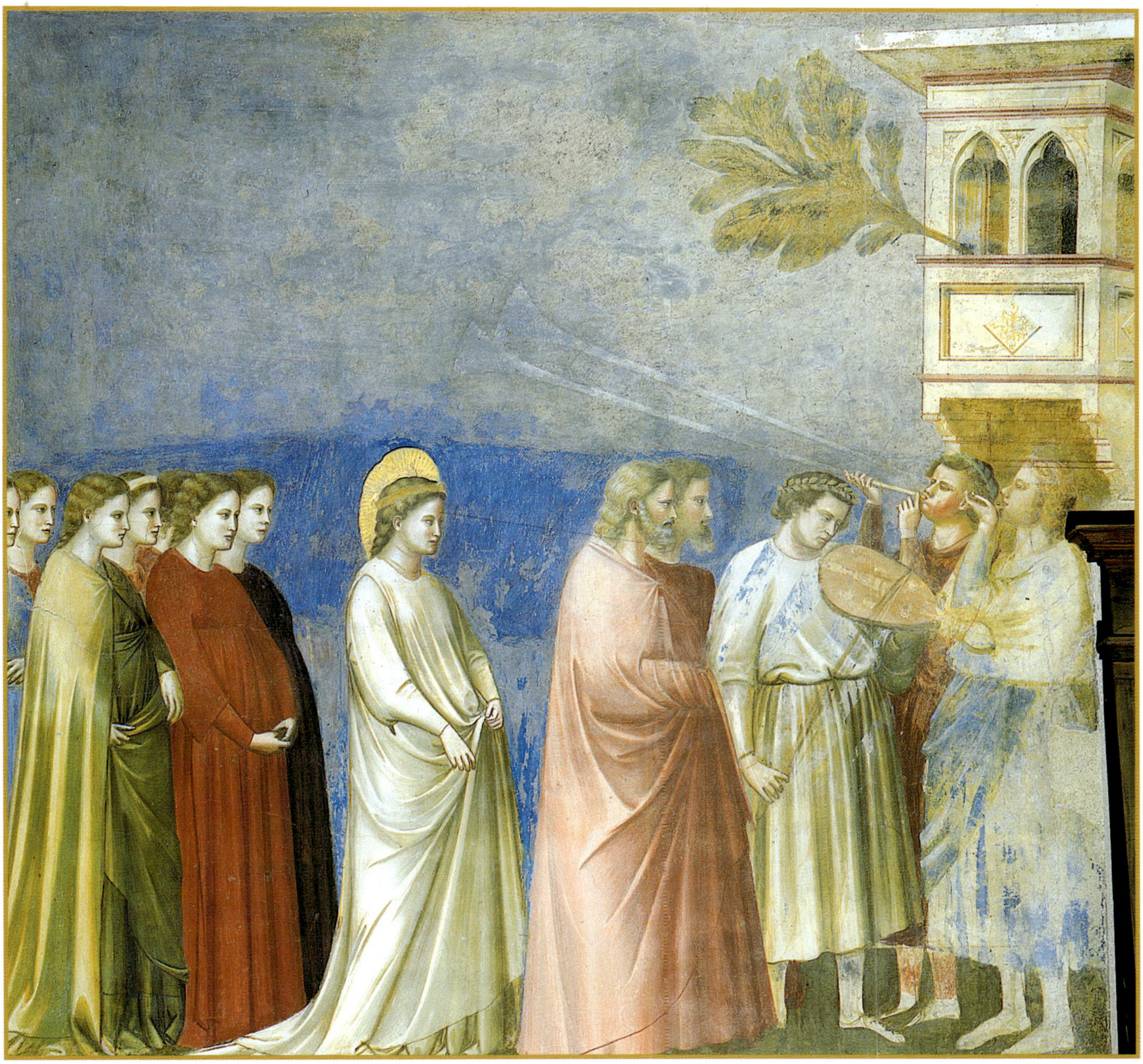

12. Mary returns to Nazareth

Still wearing her bridal gown with its long train, Mary is at the center of a cortege proceeding to the house of Nazareth (as we can see from the architectural element high up on the right: the same one that we are about to see in the Annunciation, beneath the arch of triumph). Followed by her seven friends, preceded by two temple dignitaries, she is welcomed joyously amid the music of clarion and viella, and by leaves growing green on the balcony.

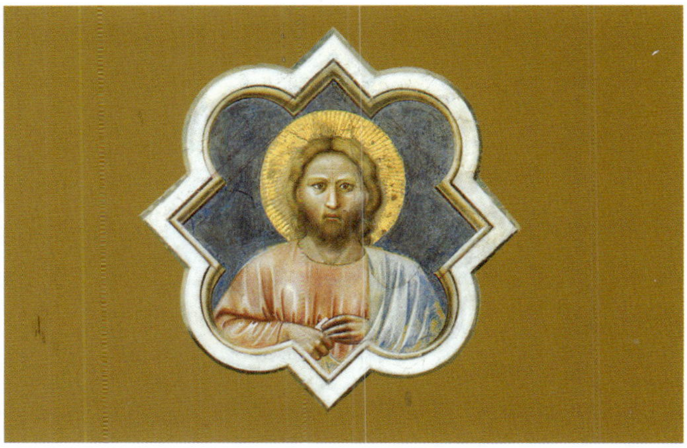

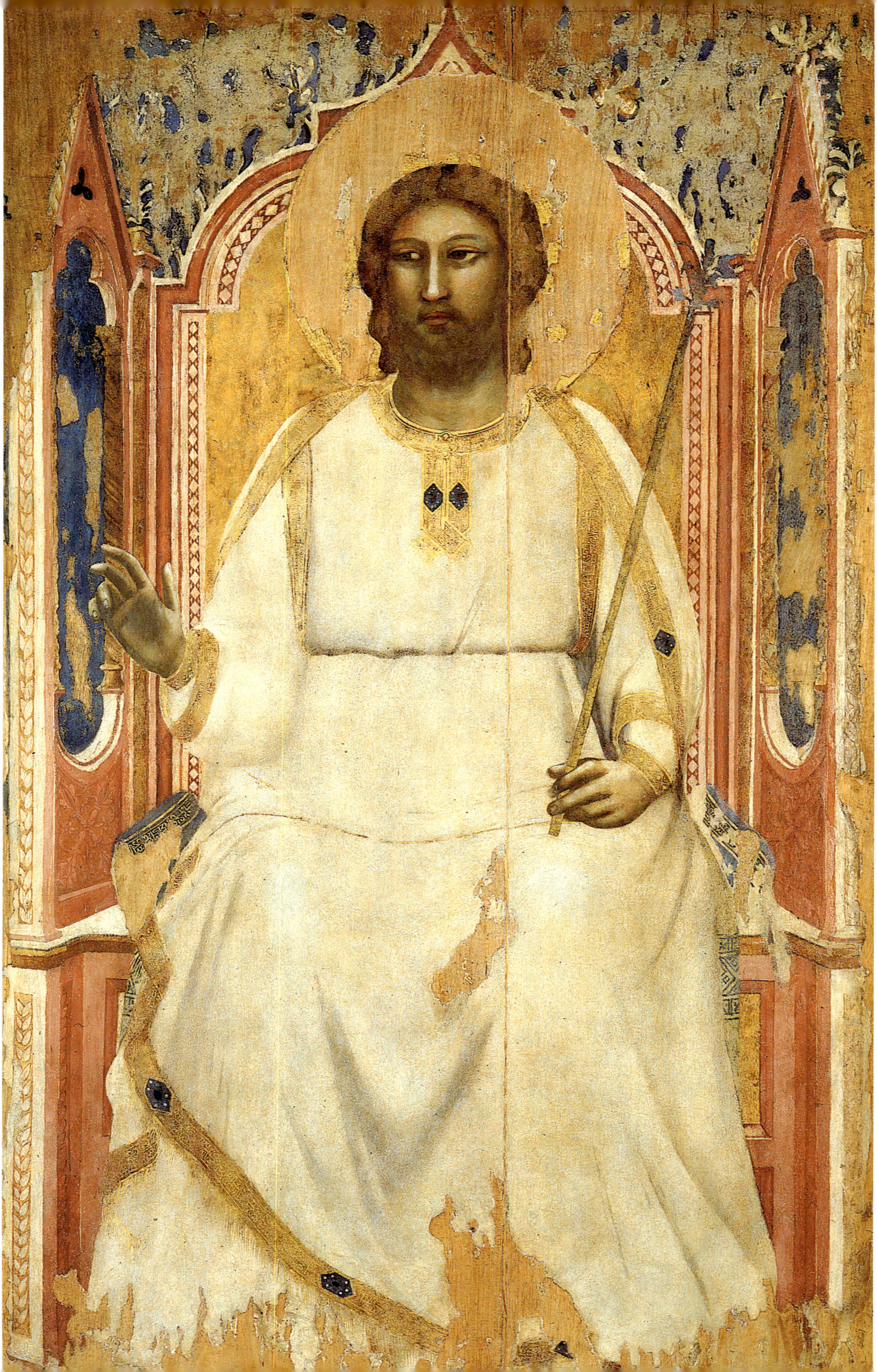

13. Arch of triumph: the Annunciation

In the high part of the triumphal arch, above three steps, sits the throne of the Eternal Father. He has the youthful, most comely face of Jesus ("whoever sees me sees the Father"). He is surrounded by angels standing in two concentric semicircles, while Gabriel stands out alone, his arms folded; on the right, he awaits orders from God. Then, on our left, the archangel himself reaches toward God, ready to accept his command.

And now we have come to the Annunciation. The angel of the Lord rises enormous on our left, in the act of bringing the news to Mary; and she — symmetrically kneeling, on the right — seems to encircle in her womb the Word (evoked by the silver book she is holding) which has been made flesh. As Bruce Cole notes, the message of the angel seems to be transmitted across the arch of the choir: arch, "parabola", that is, word which "symbolically" joins the two figures.

Here everything symbolically affirms the gratuitous initiative of God who descends and saves: the mass of red light which reaches Mary, raining down from the throne; the two curtains which, as if shaken by a wind exploding in the center, specularly move to alight on the two balconies. Then emerges the extraordinary architecture forming the background of the two symmetrical niches, in reverse and descending perspective. The fact that Giotto —150 years before Mantegna, Masaccio, Piero Della Francesca and Leon Battista Alberti —is in the early stage of Renaissance painting perspective, emerges in two "little choirs" painted right at the foot of the triumphal arch, where our human viewpoint strives to see what lies beyond. Up there, instead, on those four balconies framing the angel and Mary, the laws of perspective seem to be reversed: the lines do not seem to approach each other in an "accidental point" lying beyond the picture, as in the "little choirs"; on the contrary, everything emanates from one point – the throne of god, the Beyond — toward Mary, on the earthly level; and it seems to spread infinitely throughout the universe. (That is why we say "uni-verse": the totality of reality converging into unity; since "man's redeemer, Jesus Christ, is the center of the cosmos and of history").

During the second half of the twentieth century, scholars have emphasized the "exceptional effect of spatial illusion aroused by the two small choirs" (G. Basile), the "play of perspective" (P. Toesca), "the effect of truth in illusion" (R. Longhi): this is what enthuses the modern observer. But they have also noted "the accidental point inverted with respect to that of the twin niches in which stand the two persons of the *Annunciation*, in the upper part of the triumphal arch" (Basile). Now, undoubtedly the Lady of the Annunciation to whom the chapel is dedicated stands at the center of Giotto's interst. Here, he affirms, not the gaze of man striving toward mystery (the little choirs), but the gaze of God descending toward man, creating and recreating man and allowing him to recognize his creatural, redeemed identity: "I am You who make me"; I consist of You, oh Lord, who create me. The reversed perspective of so many Russian ikons — just think of the famous *Trinity* by Rublev — follows this direction.

On one precise day, the good Mystery that makes all things became an embryo and a fetus in the womb of that young girl, "and lives among us": with her, "full of grace", we all receive grace. Here is the event that cuts history in two. March 25: the Event of the Incarnation.

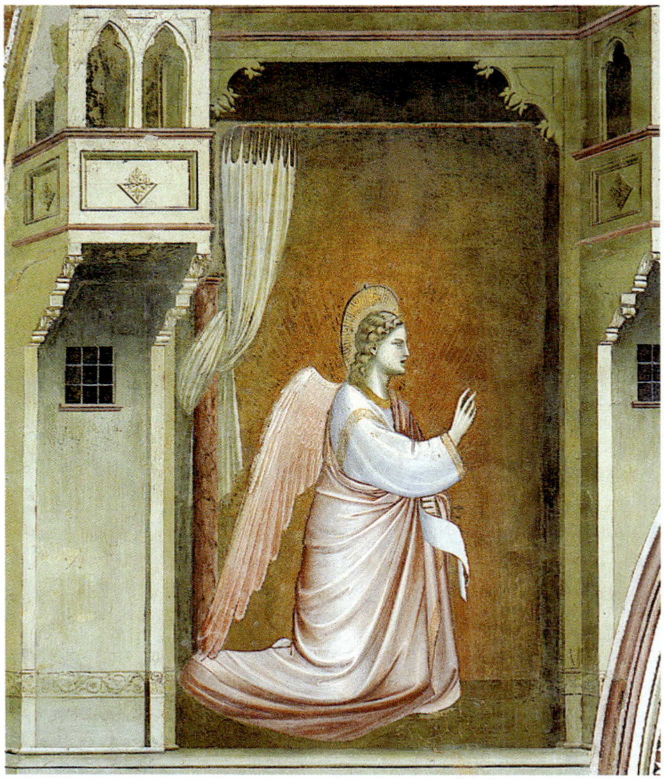

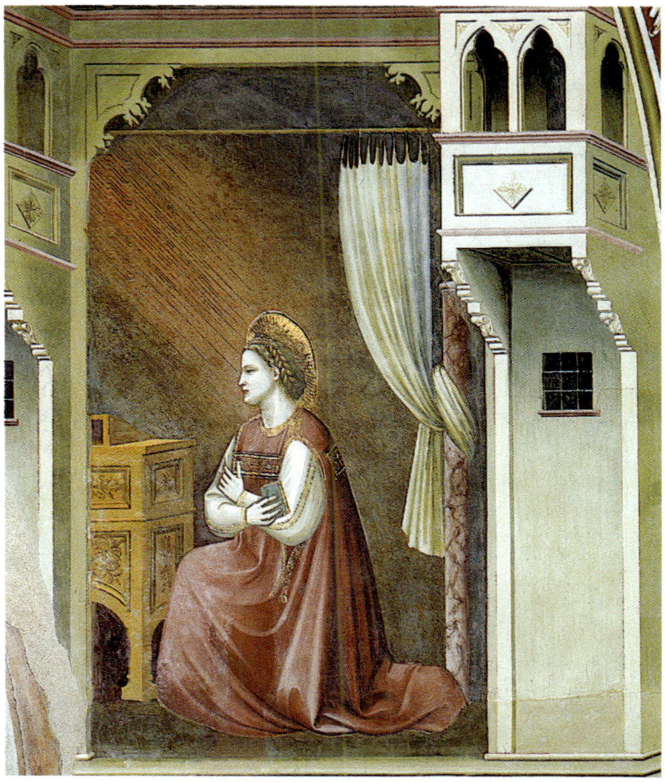

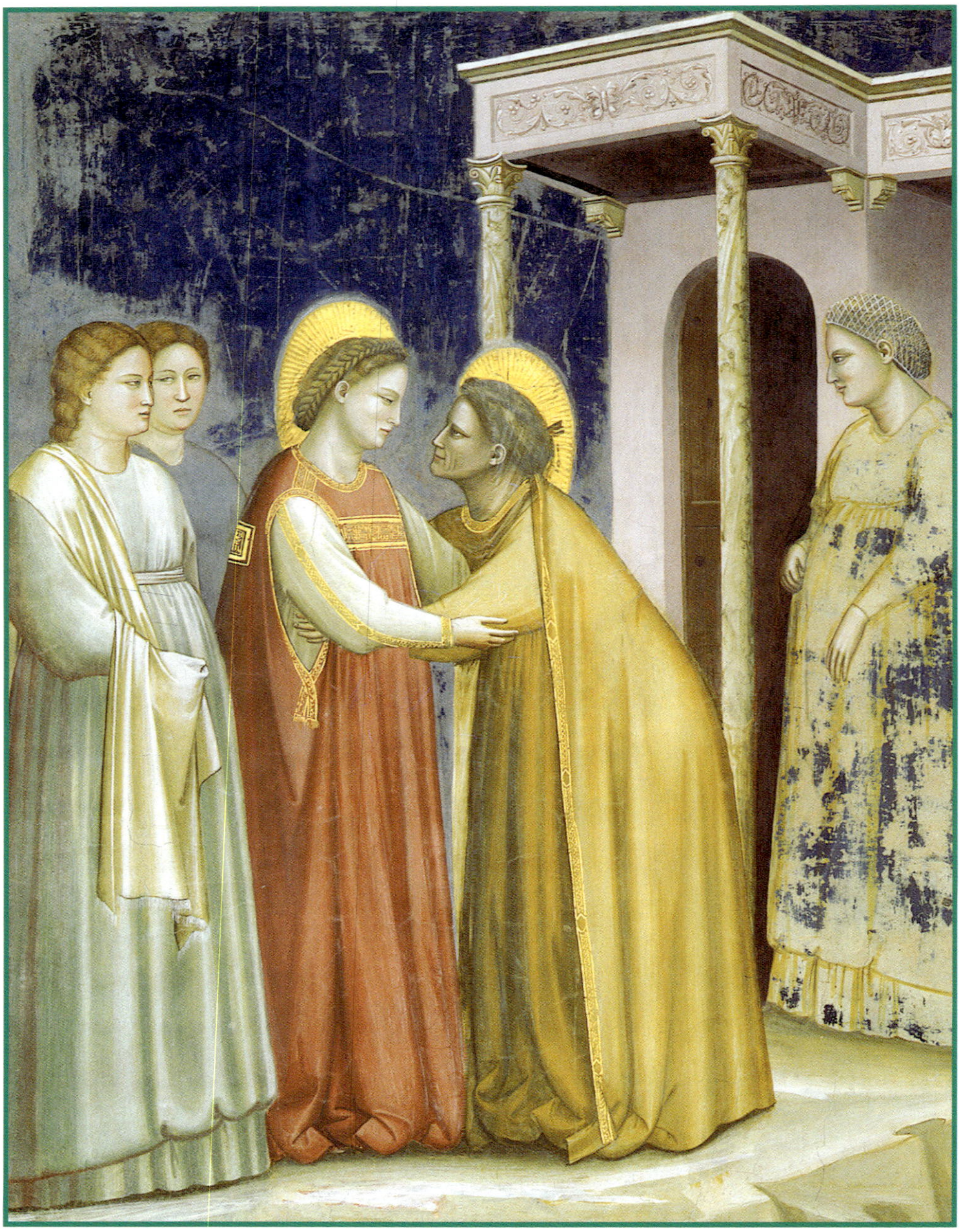

14. Mary visits St. Elizabeth

The first fruits of divine Charity which in the annunciation becomes flesh in the womb of the virgin, is the charity of Mary who travels around 150 kilometers in order to visit her cousin, Elizabeth, together with two handmaidens, one of whom carries a cloth belt as a gift. Thus begin the stories of Jesus' infancy and public life, which will end symmetrically at the other pillar of the triumphal arch, with the *Betrayal of Judas*.

Elizabeth leaves the house to meet Mary. She bends toward her a face marked by the years: like Sarah, the wife of Abraham, like Anna, the wife of Joachim, she, too, remains pregnant when she is elderly, by a grace of God announced by the angel to her husband, Zachariah. Their arms entwine; in the womb of the two women Jesus and John the Baptist recognize one another and take up a secret dialogue. Maria breaks into song, the *Magnificat*.

She is wearing the same gold-bordered, red bridal over-gown that she wore in the picture above, on the day of the Annunciation (the hairdo encircling her head like a garland also marks her as a married woman). Here is the one "full of grace", totally enrobed in the Charity of God. Her robe, partly covered by the blue cape (whose blue tint, applied on a dry surface, has mostly fallen away), is worn by her, as well, in the four following scenes: *Nativity, Epiphany, Presentation at the temple, Flight to Egypt*.

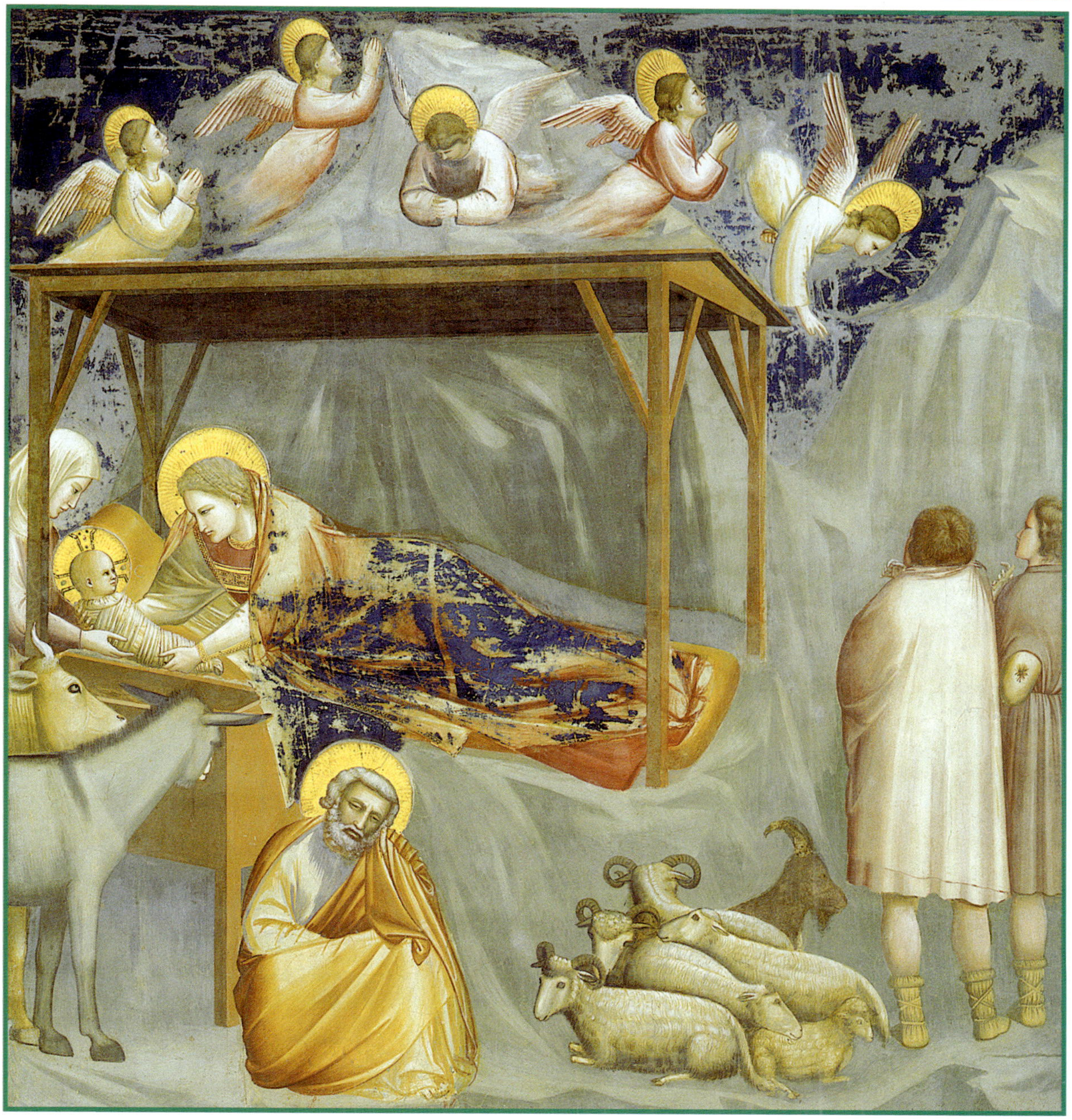

15. Nativity

In the Nativity scene a quiet joy pervades the Event. Above the little hut a flight of angels forms an arch, and then descends, bringing the news to the shepherds; all of the sheep are sleeping except one, which watches tenderly over its little lamb. Near a little donkey with outstretched neck, an ox intensely stares at the Event. Above, the midwife and the Mother close the circle, laying the newborn baby in the manger. Mary seems to be thrusting her son towards an altar.

In the reciprocal attraction between his gaze and her gaze lies the focal point of the scene, within the rocking, cradle-like space created for the babe by the arms of the two women (in analogy with the *Last Supper* of the lower area, whose focal center, symmetrically and on the left of the picture, is John's head lying against Jesus' bosom).

On the front plane, a bit distant from the manger, sits St. Joseph. As described by St. Bonaventure, he is quite sad; his eyes are half-closed in regret at not having found a more amenable place for the birth of God's son. We shall see him again in the *Epiphany* and — once more, a bit detached — in *Presentation at the temple* and *Flight to Egypt*: a man bearing, like us, original sin, he thus incarnates virginity; there is "a profound distance [...] in his absolute nearness to Mary", since "the vocation for virginity is a gift implying an inner detachment, an inner pain" (L. Giussani).

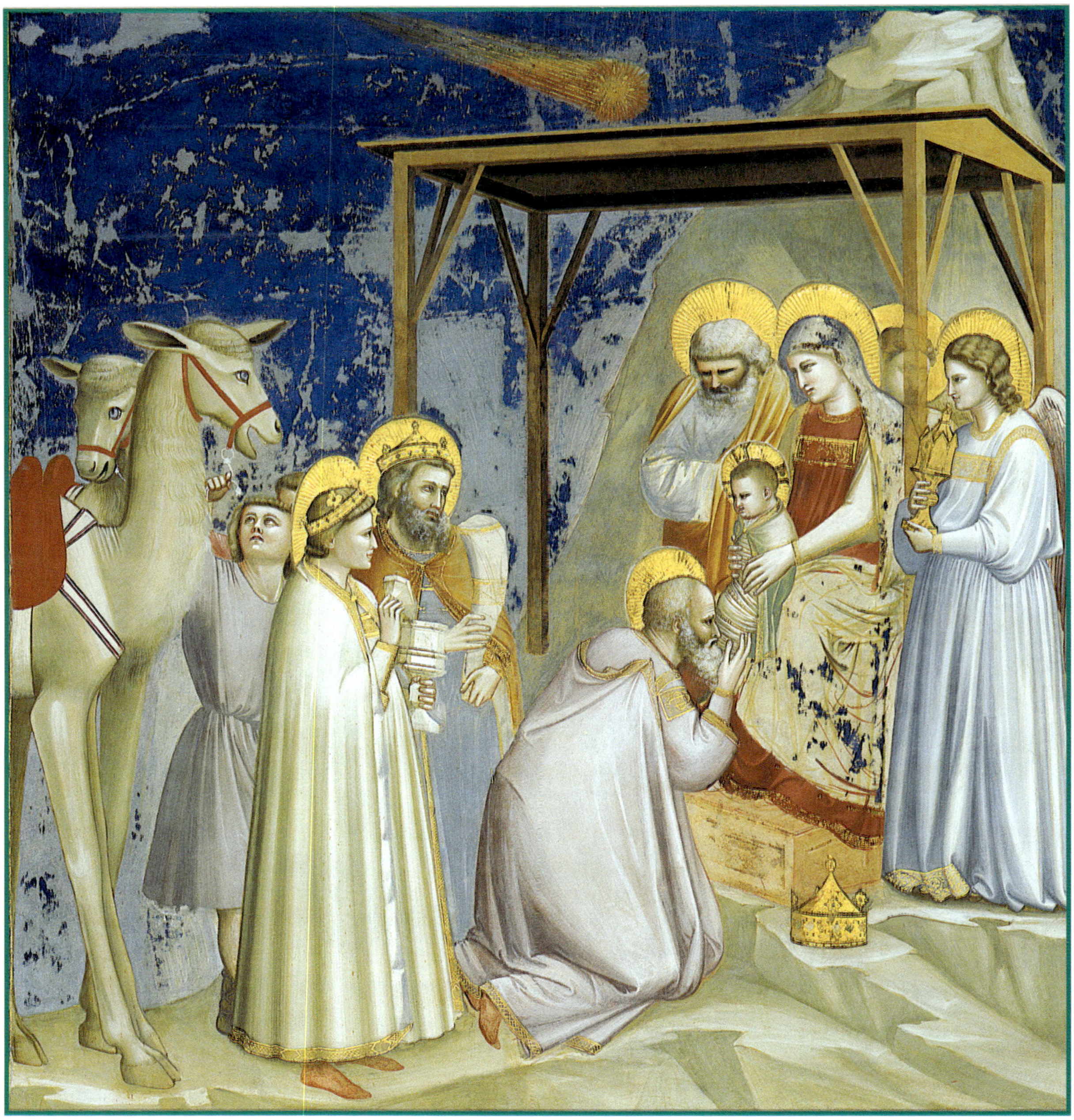

16. Epiphany
Here is the same hut appearing in the Nativity, but shifted toward the right, and changed into a humble sort of baldachin over the throne of the "king of the Jews". At his feet the first of the three Kings has laid his crown, and kneels in adoration (in the lower area of the Chapel paintings, this gesture finds correspondence in the figure of Jesus, who bows over the feet of Peter, in the Washing of the feet; as it does in the figure of Anna, in the upper area, who kneels to receive her "annunciation"). The emotional vibration of his gaze is unforgettable.
On the right, an angel holds the gift of gold in a monstrance evoking the mystery of the Eucharist instituted in the *Last Supper*. Our gaze once more descend to the Last Supper, repeated twice — symmetrically —underneath the hut.
Above, the "star" that the Magi have followed is realistically represented as a comet. On the left, the dromedary, its mouth and blue eye wide open, contemplates the Event in wonder. Everything — heaven and earth, the human world and the animal, shepherds and kings — converges toward the Child, the King of the universe. Thanks to that Fact, it is, indeed, "uni-verse".

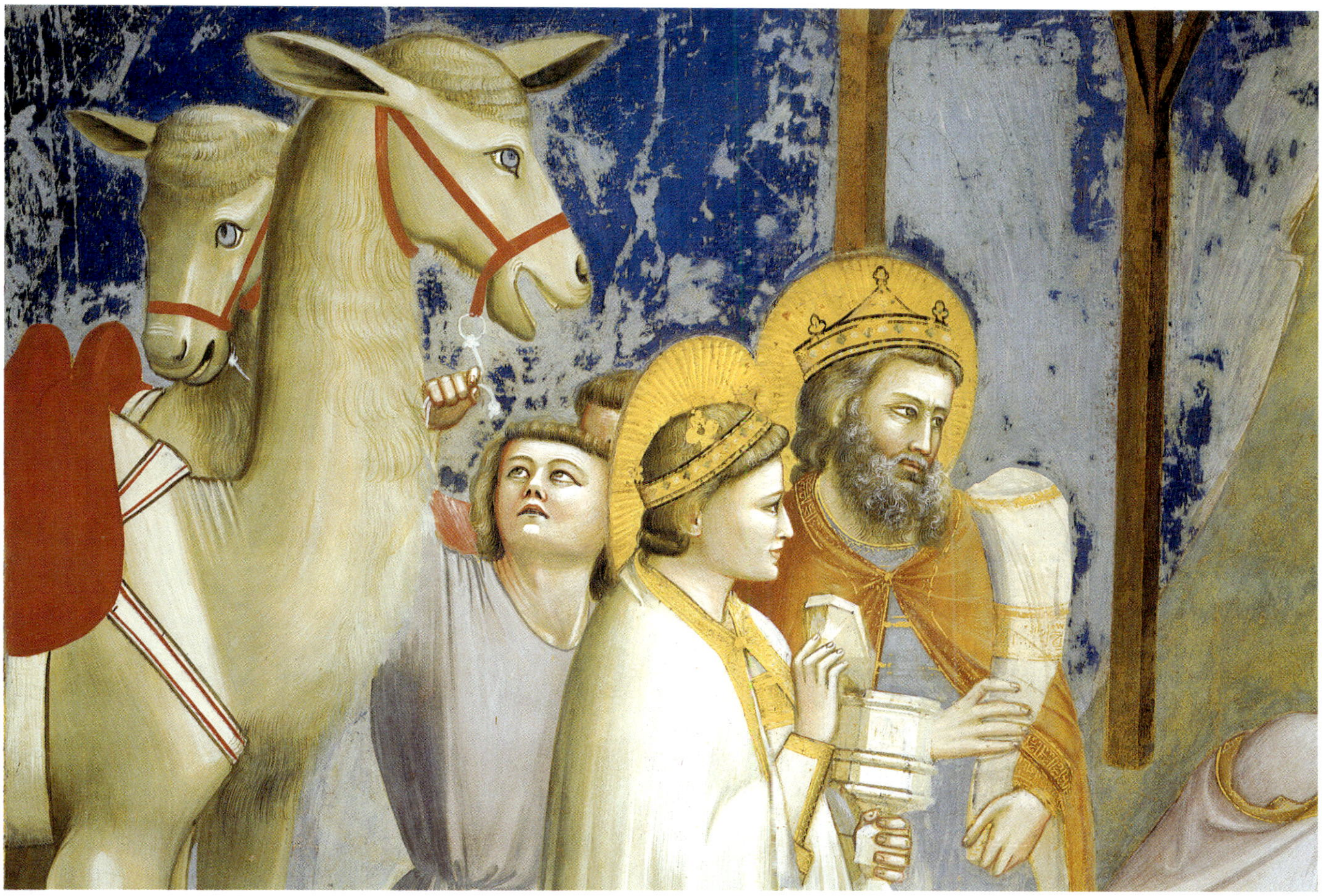

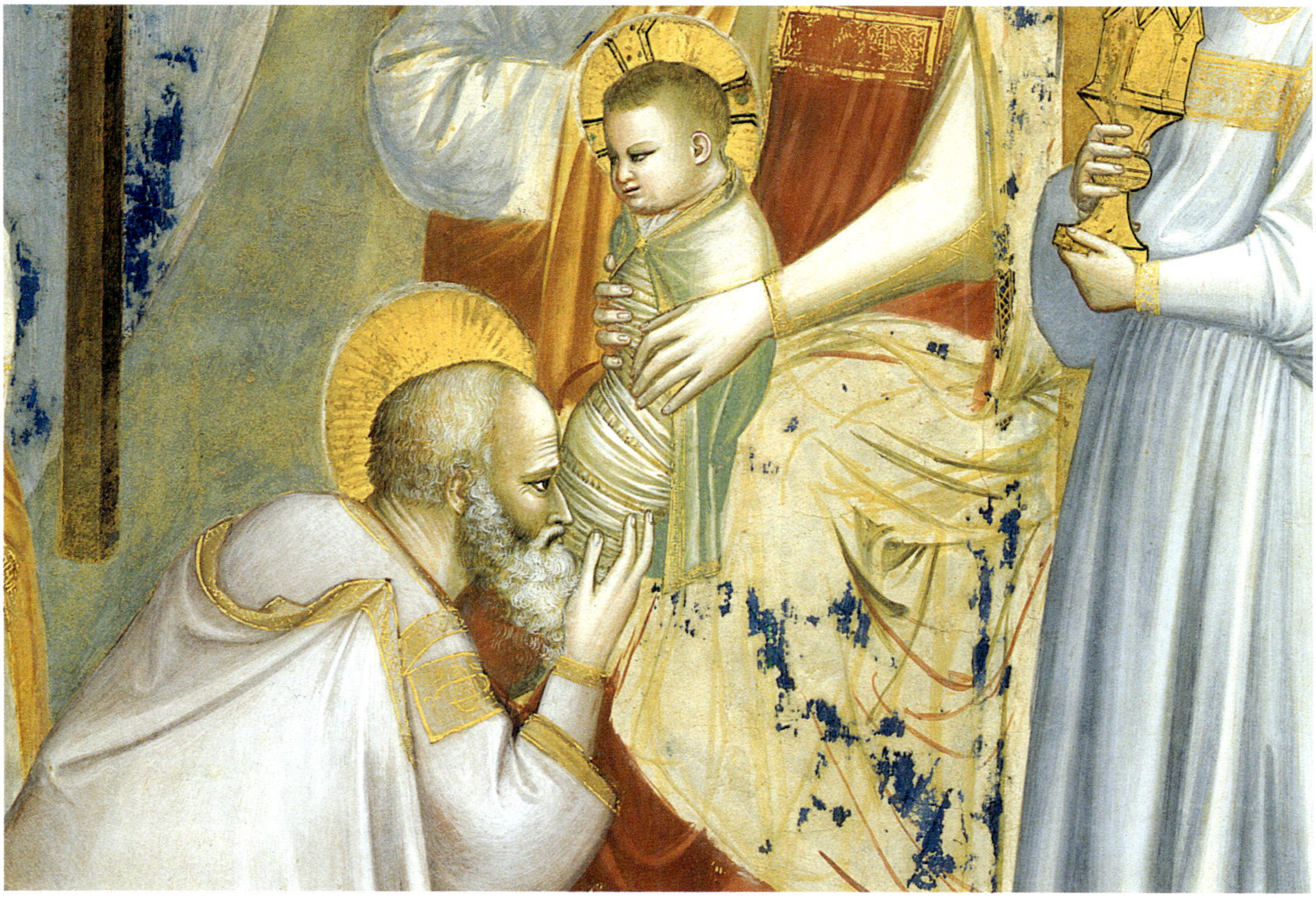

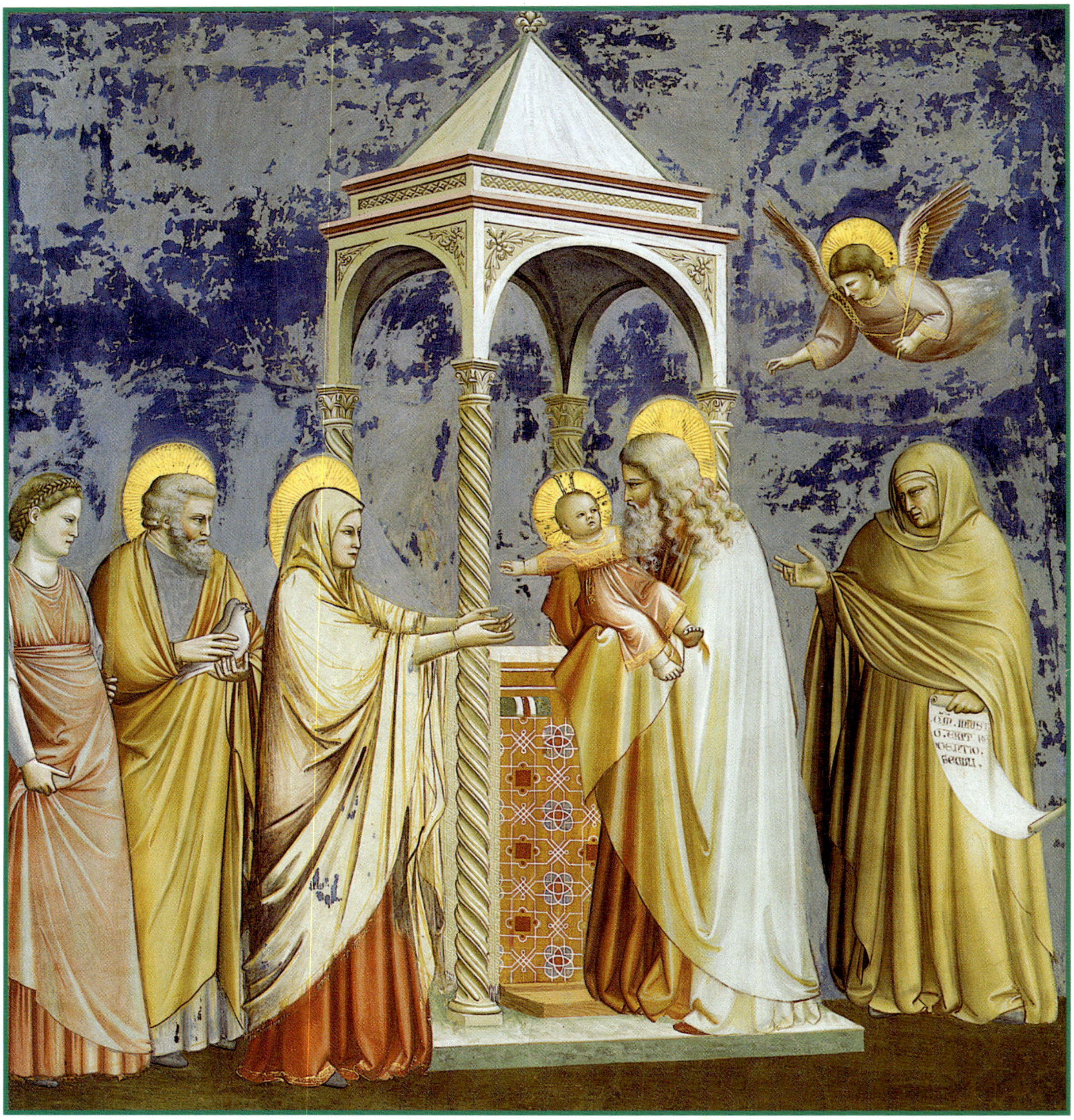

17. Presentation of the baby Jesus at the temple
"Ipapante", or "Encounter" (this is the ancient Oriental name of the feast): the encounter between the awaiting of Israel (and of every true man) and its fruition; "candelora" is the feast name which arose in Gaul, and which is dear to the people: the luminous procession of candles.
Giotto sets this great feast on stage, which closes the Nativity celebrations and opens the way to Easter; in word-for-word closeness he follows the gospel of Luke, 2:22-40. In obedience to the law of Moses, Mary and Joseph proceed to the temple in order to consecrate their first-born to the Lord; Joseph offers a pair of turtledoves in sacrifice. The temple framing the baby Jesus is the same tabernacle from which Joachim was driven, and at which the child Mary was presented: a "spatial cell" repeated three times. On the altar lies the same cloth that we say facing us in the scenes preparatory to the wedding of Mary and Joseph (*Consignment of the twigs* and *Prayer for the flowering of the twigs*).
Giotto leads our glance to the eyes of Simeon and Jesus, who are looking at one another. The old man, he who had spent his life awaiting "Israel's consolation", can now contemplate it and take it into his arms. Now, he says, I can go in peace, "for my eyes have seen"; the "salvation" and the "light" are this child in flesh and blood, that I can touch, and that I worship. Simeon's hands are hidden underneath his cape, in an act of supreme reverence, of respectful detachment.

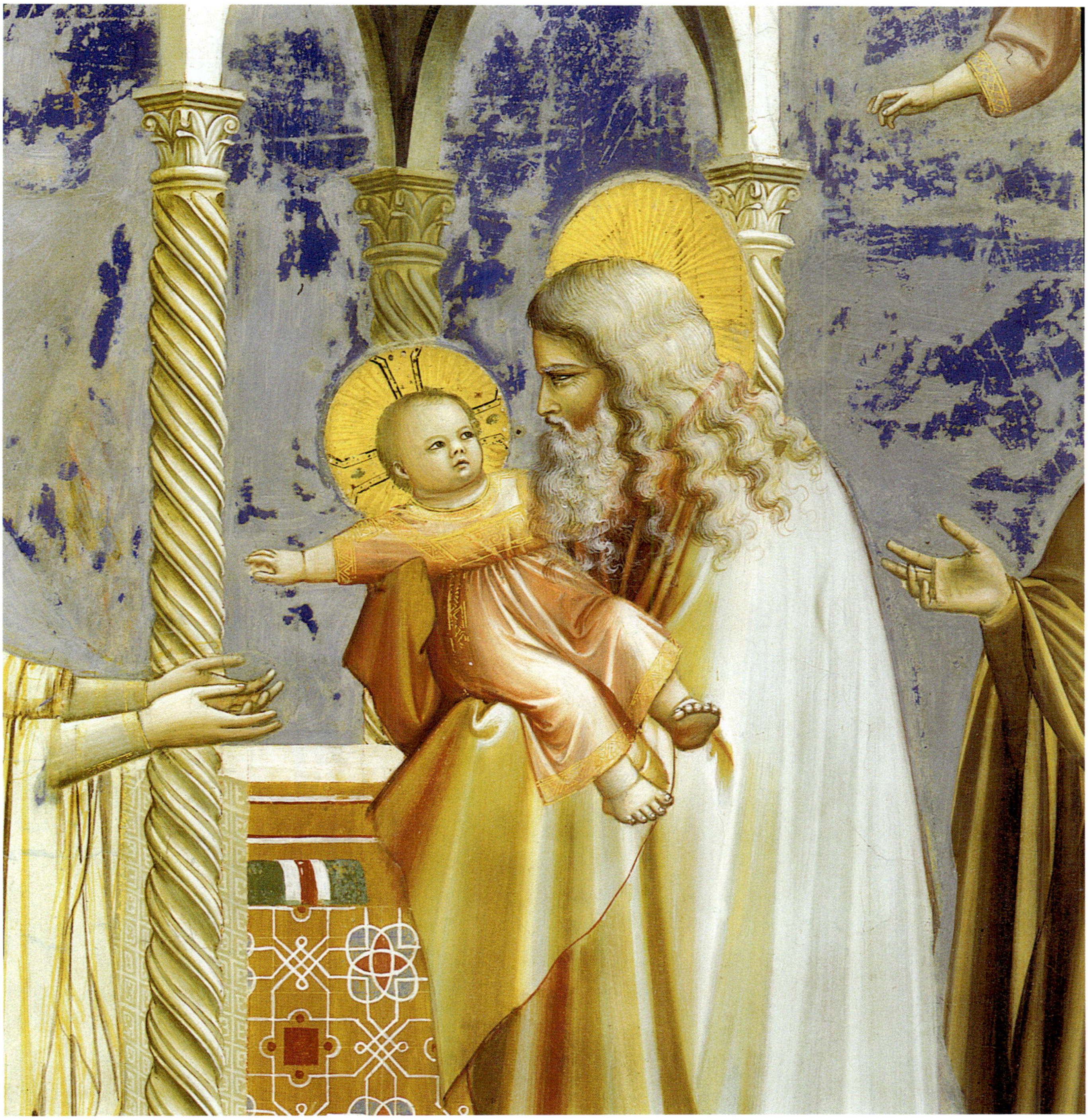

Both the eighty-four-year old prophetess Anna and the angel above her point to the child with their right hand, who in turn points to his mother. Mary's hands consign that creature, so intimately hers and so intimately of an Other (in Italian, the element "sign" coexists both in consegnare, to consign, and insegnare, to point to). The mother's hands and those of the son seek out each other, but with detachment. "He is already going away", thinks the woman to herself, whose infinite wonderment seems soaked in quiet pain: "and a sword will pierce your soul". Jesus is already on his way to Golgotha. The kingly glory of that Child will pass by way of the cross: but his destiny is glory and peace for a promise which has reached fruition, as suggested by the thin caduceus held in the angel's hand. Here is why each evening, the Church suggests that we recite at the end of the day that true hymn to *completion* which is *Simeon's Canticle*. His eyes have seen, his hands have touched: this is reality, not abstraction.

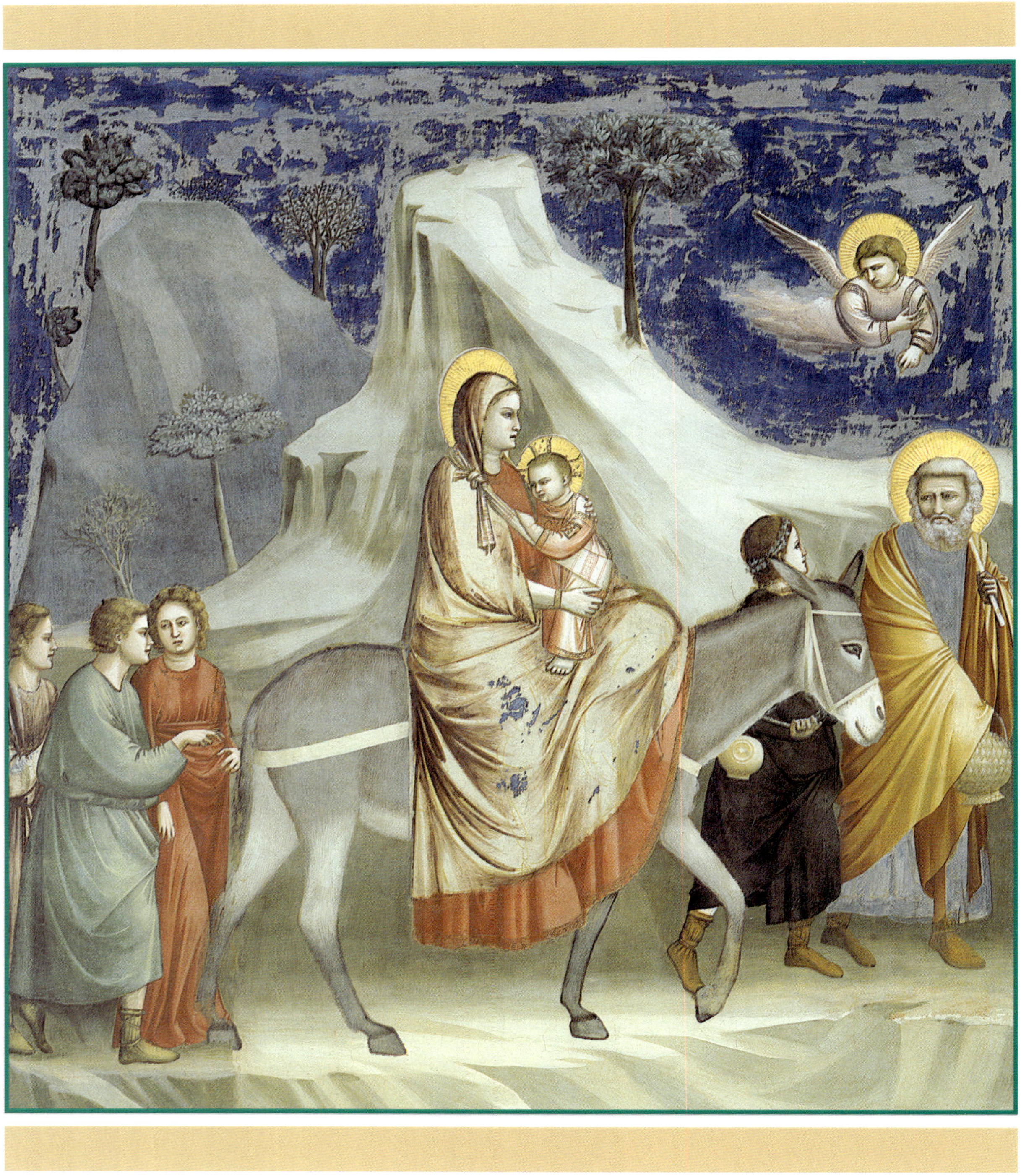

18. Flight to Egypt
Everything seems to proceed swiftly towards the right, towards salvation far from Herod: the wide swathes of the various figures, some of whose shoulders are curved in hasty movement; Joseph, who turns back in worry; the angel who points out the way to the young girl crowned with ivy, leading the donkey.
Even the rocky cliff line, which perfectly frames the Holy Family, seems to accompany their swift movement forward. The same animal world present in Epiphany appears, alongside the mineral world. All of reality participates in History.
The mother, erect in her composure, confidently holds the baby, who is protected as in a nest by the cloth band cradling him. The way is dangerous: it skirts an abyss. But angels and people watch over the Child.

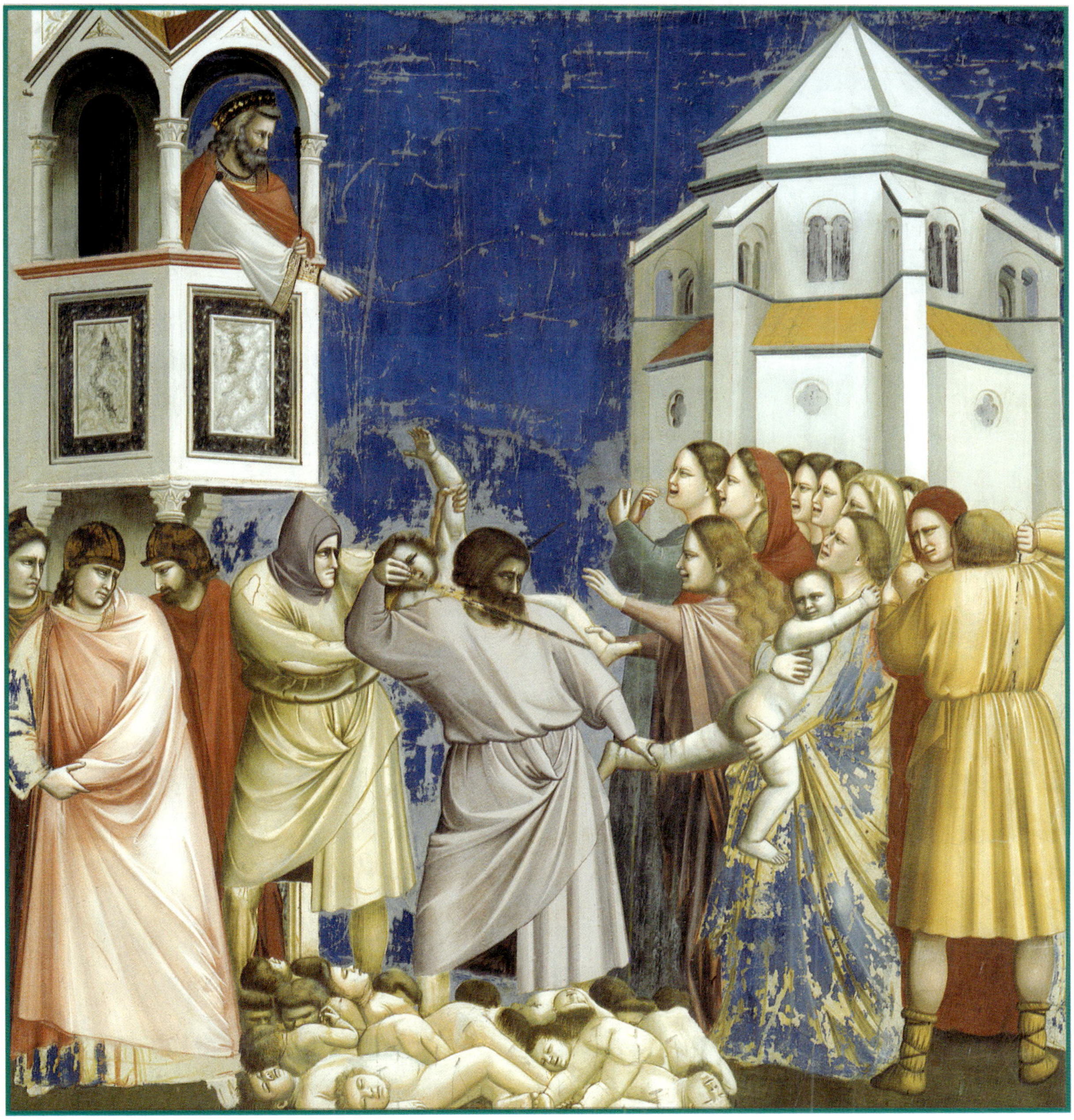

19. Slaughter of the innocents
Herod, framed by the sinister balcony of his palace, orders the slaughter of the innocents, while on the left an ecclesiastical building seems to frame and embrace the heart-rending pain of the mothers. (Its form probably recalls the apse of San Francesco, in Bologna; or perhaps resembles an octagonal baptistery, or the basilica of the Nativity, in Bethlehem.)
The focal point of the painting — at the cross point of diagonals — is the malevolent head of a hired assassin. In carrying out Herod's orders, with one hand he grabs hold of the baby (it clasps its mother, who is dressed in blue, like Mary) and with the other, brandishes a spike as if to pierce it. The pitiless, oblique-descending dynamics proceeding from Herod to his killer are opposed by the little arm of another creature, stretched out toward the king in involuntary supplication; this baby, too, is about to be killed, by a second thug. A third soldier, on the extreme right, is tearing a child from its mother's arms; but the three figures on extreme left seem moved by the vision of all those poor little christs, with their sides pierced. One man, dressed in red, is unable to stand the sight, and looks elsewhere.

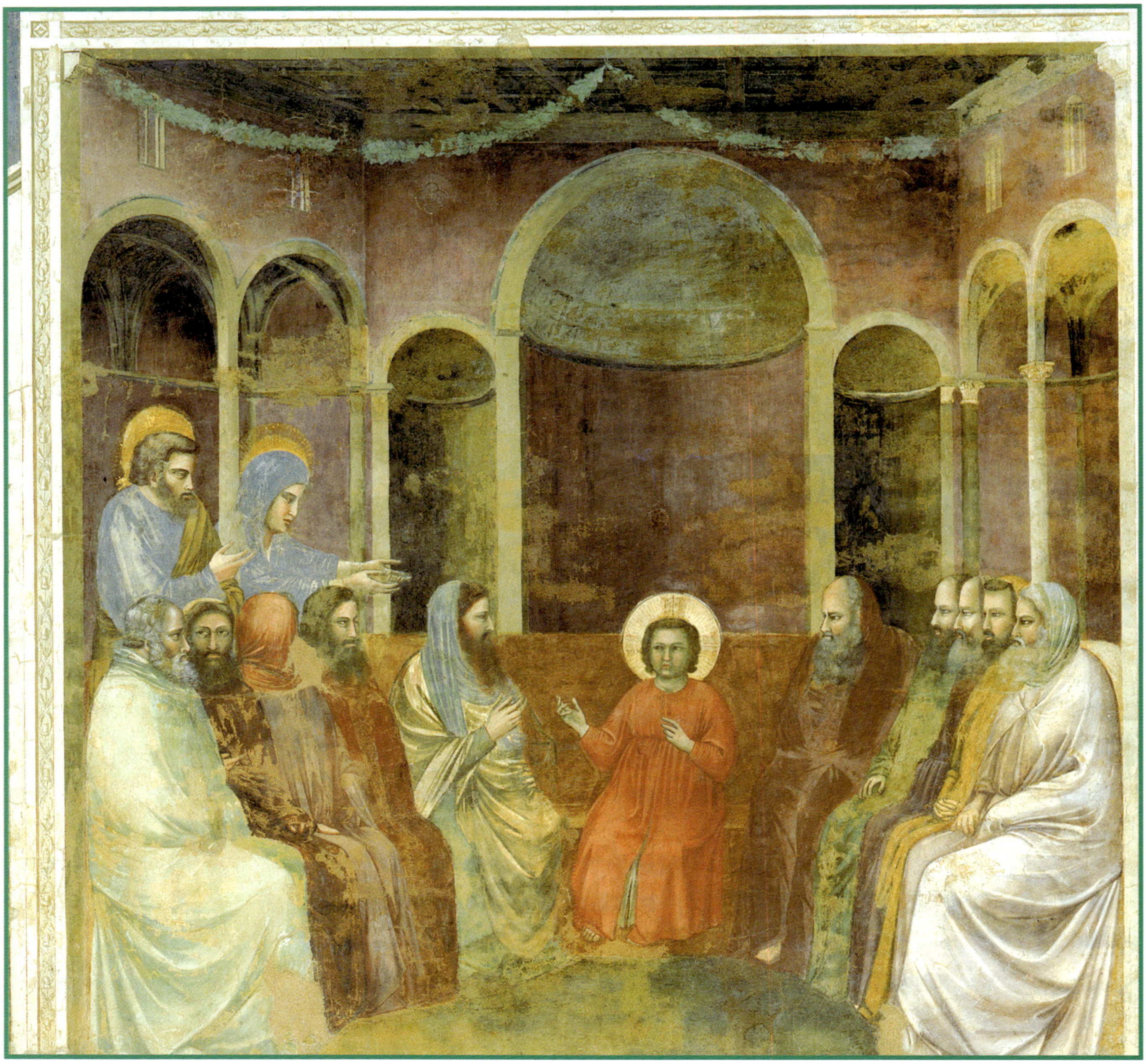

20. Jesus among the temple rabbis

The twelve-year-old boy has got lost in Jerusalem, where he has gone with his parents to celebrate Passover. Mary and Joseph look for him in anguish. They find him among the rabbis, in the temple.

The sacred hall is adorned with garlands for the feast. The arches, seven in all (a Biblical number, dear to the Jews), frame the groups and single figures. Within the great apse arch, in perspective with the sancta sanctorum, he is there, the boy with a halo, all dressed in "divine" red, from which faintly emerges the "human" blue. He is surrounded by a half-circle of ten doctors of the law, "full of wonder at his intelligence" (and ten is the number of Moses' commandments). Standing on our left (but on Jesus' right), are Mary and Joseph; they have just entered, and their faces are tense. A rabbi turns to look at them. The hands of the mother and putative father stretch out toward the son, but he seems to suggest, with his right index finger, "my Father" in heaven. The pain of loss, the joy of finding again. Joy ever more laden "with an inner detachment, with inner pain".

The eighteen years that follow can only be imagined, as we "see" him growing "in wisdom, age and grace", a young carpenter in Nazareth. A seemingly insignificant life.

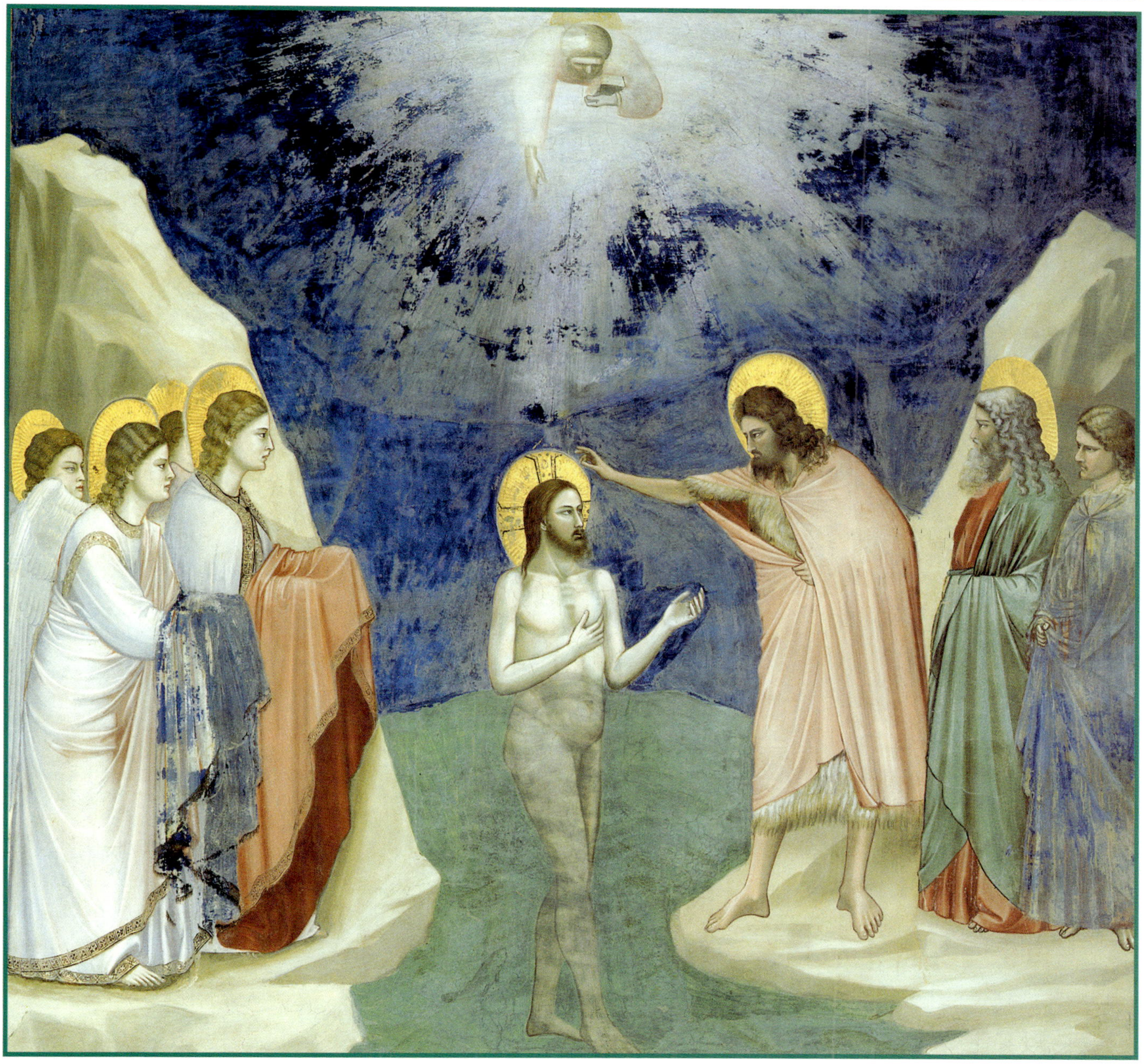

21. Baptism of Jesus
At "around thirty years" of age Jesus was baptized in the river Jordan.
The landscape behind him draws in toward that man, as if to point him out. His head is at the cross point between the trinitary verticality (a glimpse of the Father, the dove of the Spirit — now invisible — and the nude body of Christ), and the wavy horizontality of the haloes. At the exact point where the diagonals cross is Jesus' mouth: from that day on he "began his ministry".
From above rain down the words of the father: "This is my Son, the Beloved; my favor rests on him". On one side the angels hold up his clothing, the blue and the red; on the other, Andrew and the other disciple watch. At "four in the afternoon", for those two, begins the great adventure with him: a turning point in their life, whose memory remains clear, even in the detail of the hour!
"The Word became flesh, he lived among us, and we saw his glory" (1 John 1, 14). Around 100 AD the apostle John recorded what had happened to himself and to Andrew about seventy previous, beginning at four o'clock in that unforgettable afternoon, there on the Jordan.

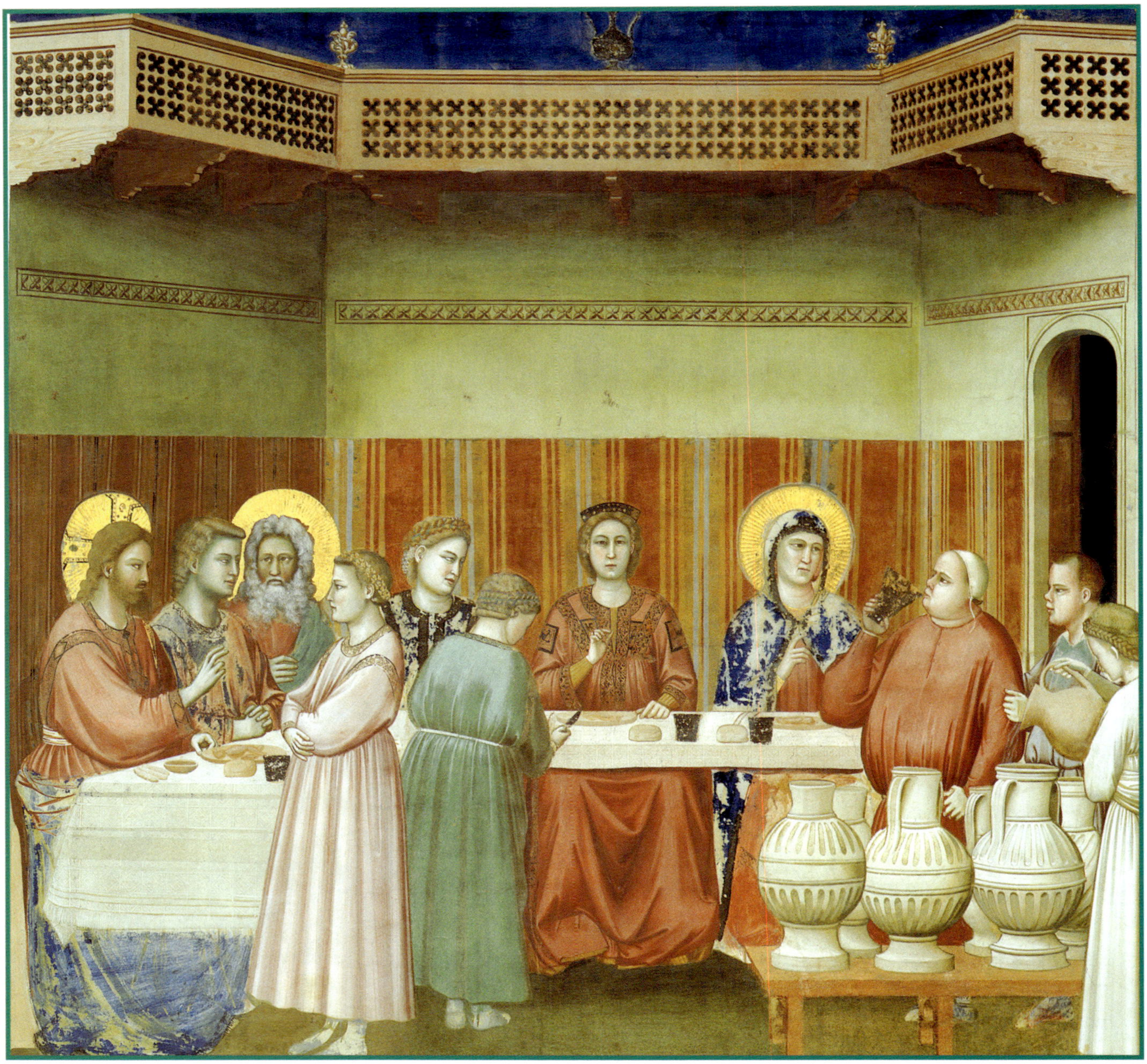

22. Wedding at Cana

Of the three years of Jesus' public life, up to the week of the Passion, Giotto depicts only two miracles, the first and the last according to the Gospel of John: the wedding at Cana and the resurrection of Lazarus.

The first is set in a fine salon, with cloverleaf designs both on the wooden loggia and the wall frieze. Sitting at table are the banqueting companions: Jesus is in the last place, the servant's place, while his first two disciples sit beside him. Commandingly, Mary turns to the servants: "Do what he tells you to". Jesus orders them to fill the six jars with water, and a maidservant obeys. The "tablemaster", big-bellied as a jar, approvingly tastes the wine, convinced that the bridegroom has kept the best wine for last: this "water which has become wine" is truly good wine. And lovely miracle it is, worked so that a feast can be a feast to the utmost degree (perhaps foreshadowing, as well, the transubstantiation of the Eucharist).

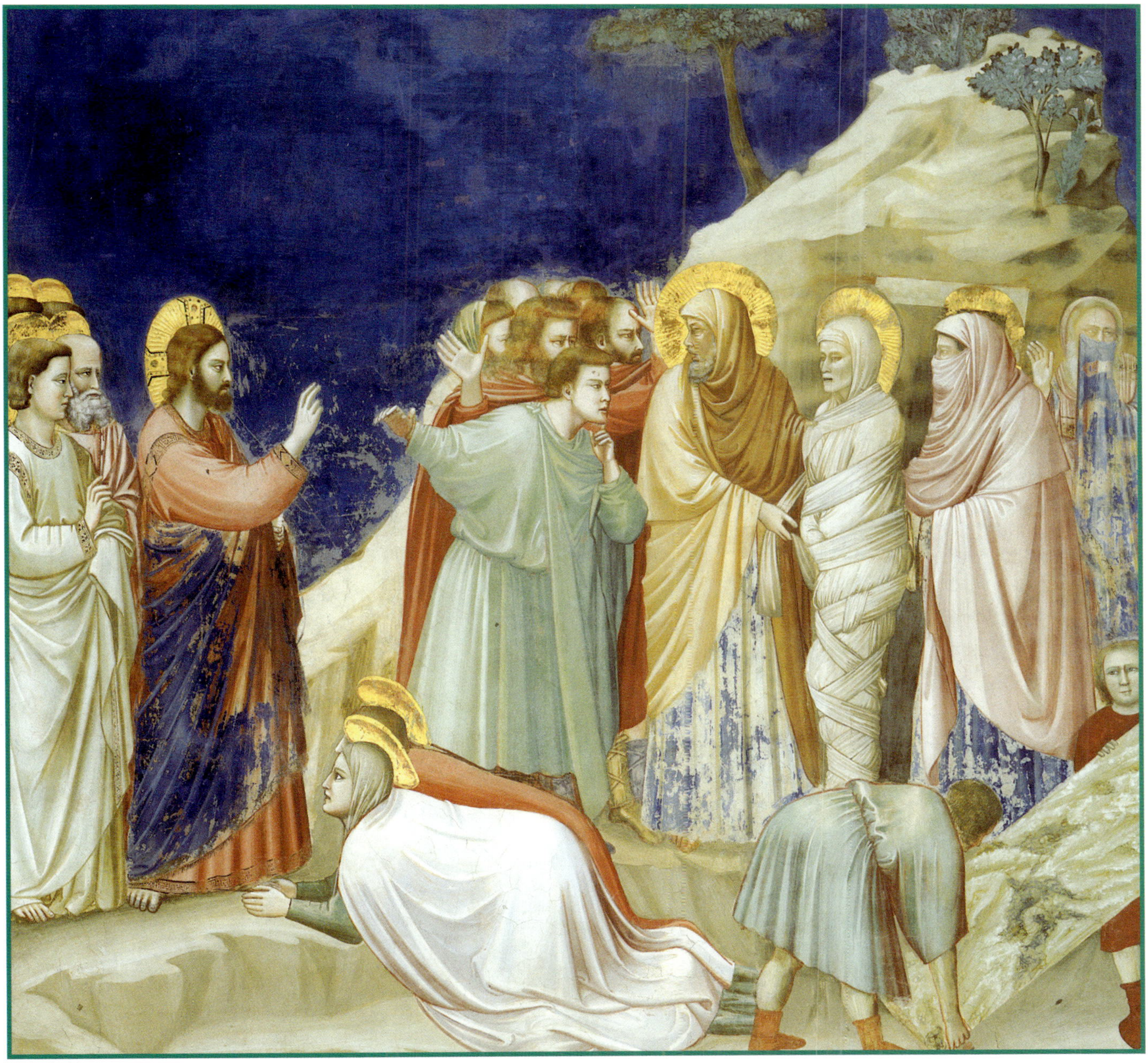

23. Resurrection of Lazarus

The potent gesture of Jesus' right hand, which we have just seen in Wedding at Cana, returns — standing out clearly against the blue background — immediately afterward, at the resurrection of Lazarus (and we shall soon see it again, in the act of blessing, on Jesus' entry into Jerusalem).

True man and true God: the man Jesus had friends "whom he greatly cherished"—Lazarus, Martha and Mary of Bethany; when he heard of Lazarus' death "he was deeply moved ... he broke into tears"; the one whom Martha recognized as the "Son of God" bears testimony to the power coming from this nature, by resurrecting his friend "who had been in the tomb for four days now". Lazarus stands there, erect; the two figures on the right cover their faces, thus showing that that body bound in a winding sheet still "gives out a bad odor"; and yet it is alive. Martha and Mary, prostrate at Jesus' feet, have made their request; he has answered; everyone is stricken and amazed; many convert, but some go off to accuse him. Consequently, on that very same day, Caiaphas and the sanhedrin "decided to put him to death".

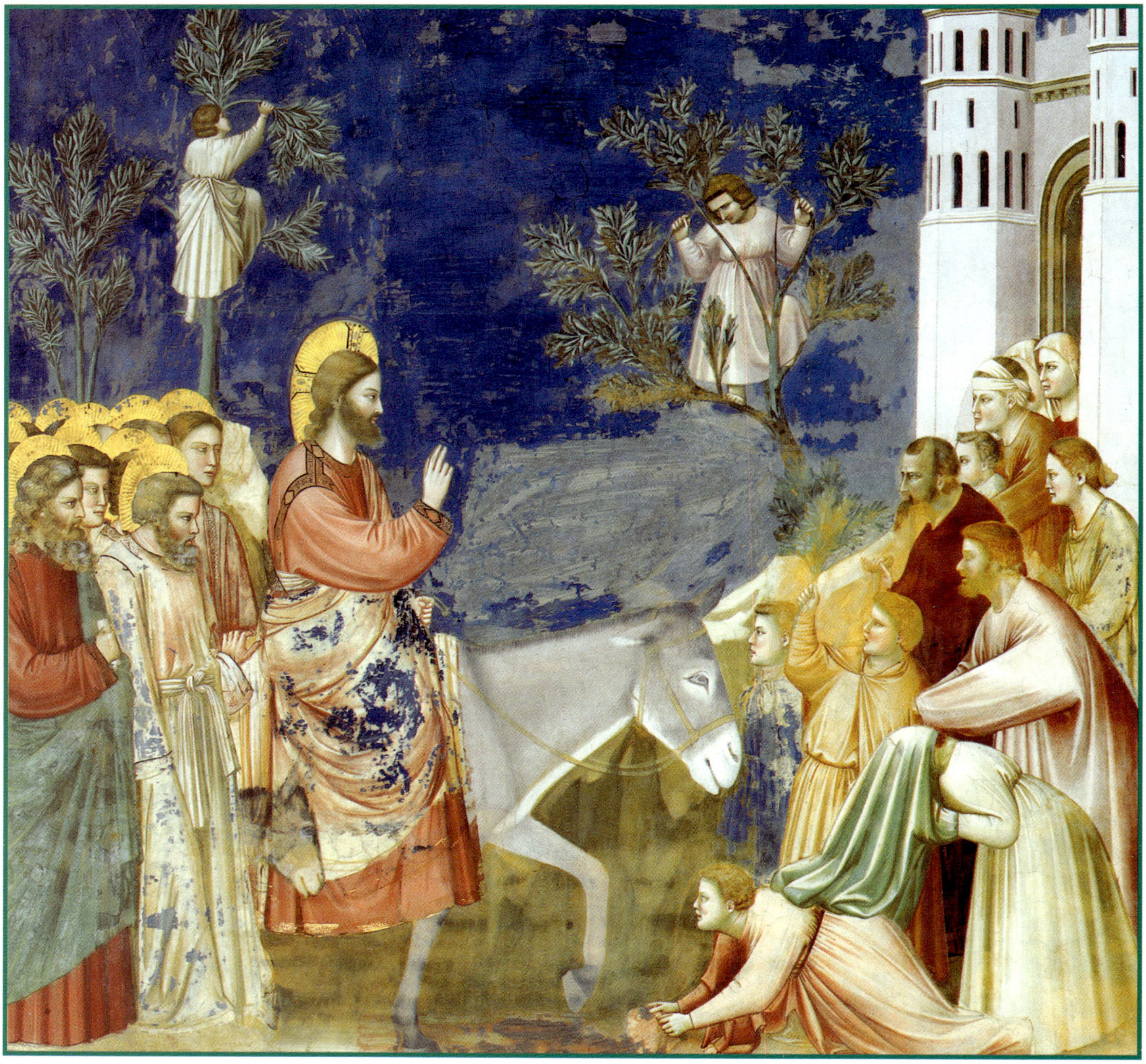

24. Jesus' entry into Jerusalem
Hailed by the exultant crowds of Jerusalem and followed by the Twelve, Jesus rises, full of dignity, on his humble mount, fulfilling the prophecy word for word (Zechariah 9:9). The donkey that had warmed the Child in Nativity, and that had taken him to Egypt with the Holy Family, appears here for the third time: the symbol of *Christus patiens*, in opposition to the steed-riding heroes, the potentates of this world as represented on so many equestrian monuments.
Jesus is about to enter the gates of Jerusalem: the same ones from which he will leave, burdened with the cross. Reads the Gospel of Mark: "Many people spread their cloaks on the road, and others greenery which they had cut in the fields". Giotto's version is, once again, literal. Three figures in particular seem to mark the photograms of a cinema sequence: from right to left, a man is beginning to take off his cloak; in front of him another, bending down, is removing his own over his head; a third, prostrate, is stretching out his cloak under the donkey's feet.

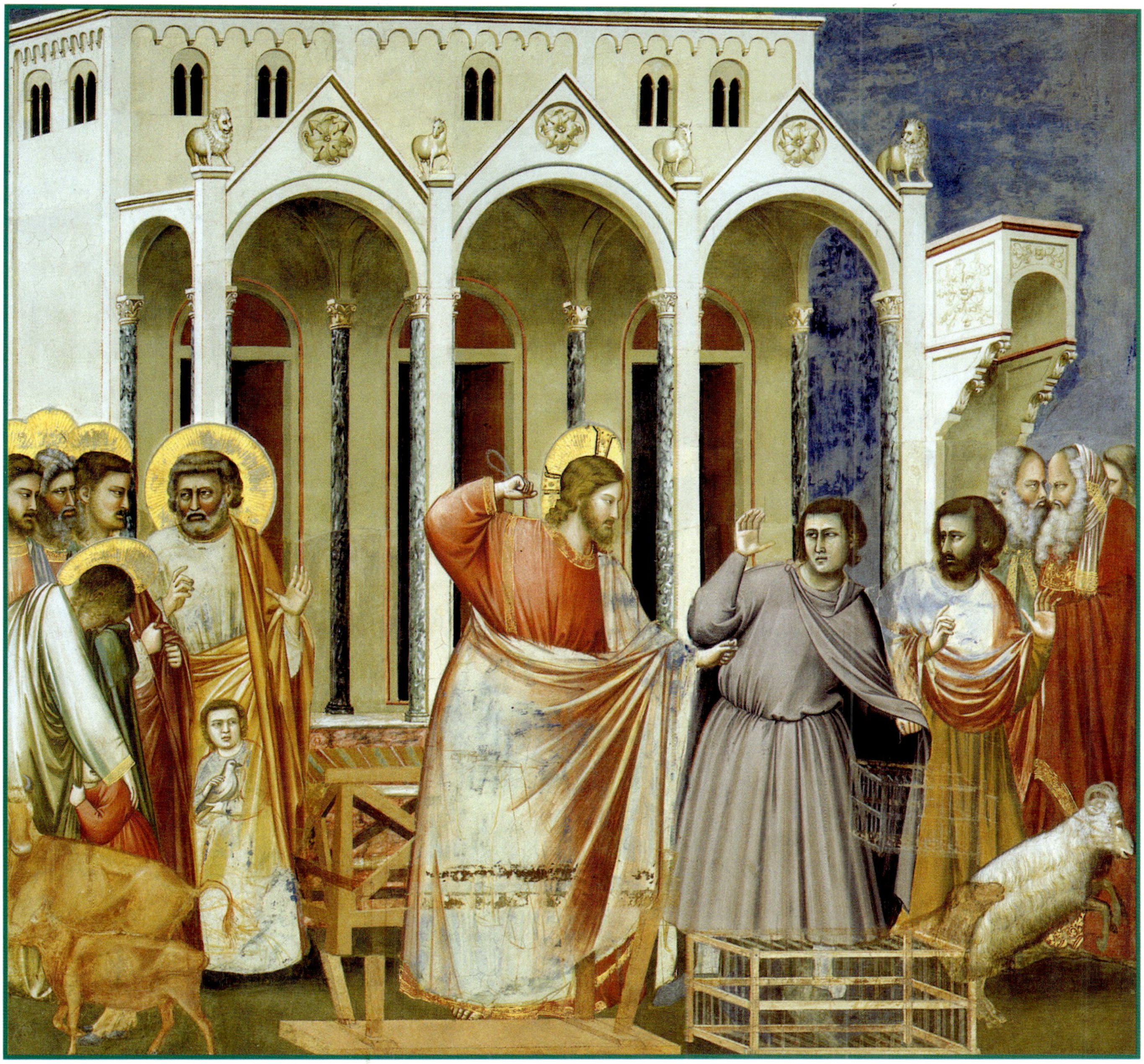

25. Expulsion of the dealers from the temple
Jesus enters the temple which has been reduced to a "thieves' den"; he "upset the tables of the money-changers and the seats of the dove-sellers". The same hand that in the three preceding pictures had worked miracles and given blessing, now comes down to scourge men, arousing a centrifugal flight of persons and animals. One apostle bends down to protect a frightened child. Another little boy, holding a dove, seems to beat his wings in mid-air, against Peter's yellow cloak: after completing this fresco, Giotto actually decided to add this child's image on a dry surface; much of the paint later fell off, creating this curious effect.
Counteropposing the group of apostles, on the far right, are the priests who had connived with the dealers — Annas, Caiaphas and another: those who after the resurrection of Lazarus had decided to put Jesus to death, now talk over how to capture him.
Jesus stands out in the center, framed by the central arch of the porch (as on the opposite end of the wall, the twelve-year-old Jesus stands out among the rabbis, within the same temple). The four columns are topped by two lions and two horses: an allusion to Venice.

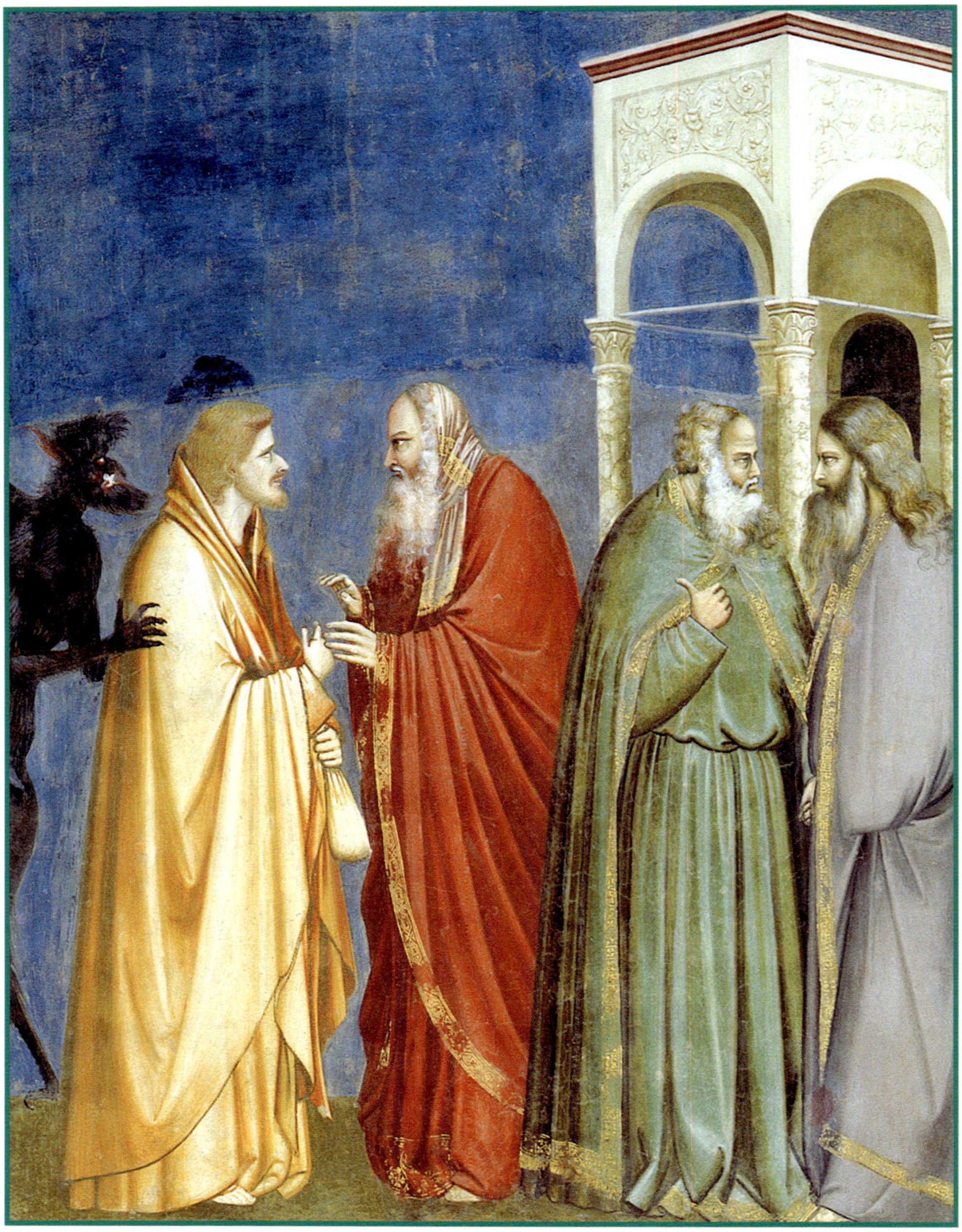

26. Betrayal by Judas
In the triumphal arch, underneath the angel Gabriel of the annunciation, is the fallen angel: a snarling, black Satan, whose profile resembles that of Judas. He lays his claws on the traitor's shoulder; Judas wears a pointed goatee, his nose is hooked, and his cloak is yellow (the color of betrayal, but also of despair; here, as in Dante, it is opposed to the green of hope). He clasps his thirty silver pieces (a miserly sum: the perfume which Mary of Bethany spread over Jesus' feet was worth 300 silver pieces! And Judas — for it was he who kept the coffers, and who "was a thief" — had complained about such wastefulness ...). The usual three priests press near him (note the colors of their clothing), in a malignant brushing of hands.

There is an evident similarity between *Betrayal of Judas* and *Mary visits St. Elizabeth*, on the other pillar of the triumphal arch; a similarity which ends up emphasizing the substantial antithesis: five figures on each side; similar colors; analogous foreshortening of the building on the right. Judas' yellowishness stands between the black of Satan (*infidelitas*) and the red of homicidal blood; on the other side, the red of Mary's charity, between the green of hope and golden faith. The two arches of the temple which frame the Simoniacs Annas and Caiaphas, are contrasted not so much by Elizabeth's house, as by Mary's womb, supported by feet solidly planted on the earth. It is the temple of the Word Incarnate.

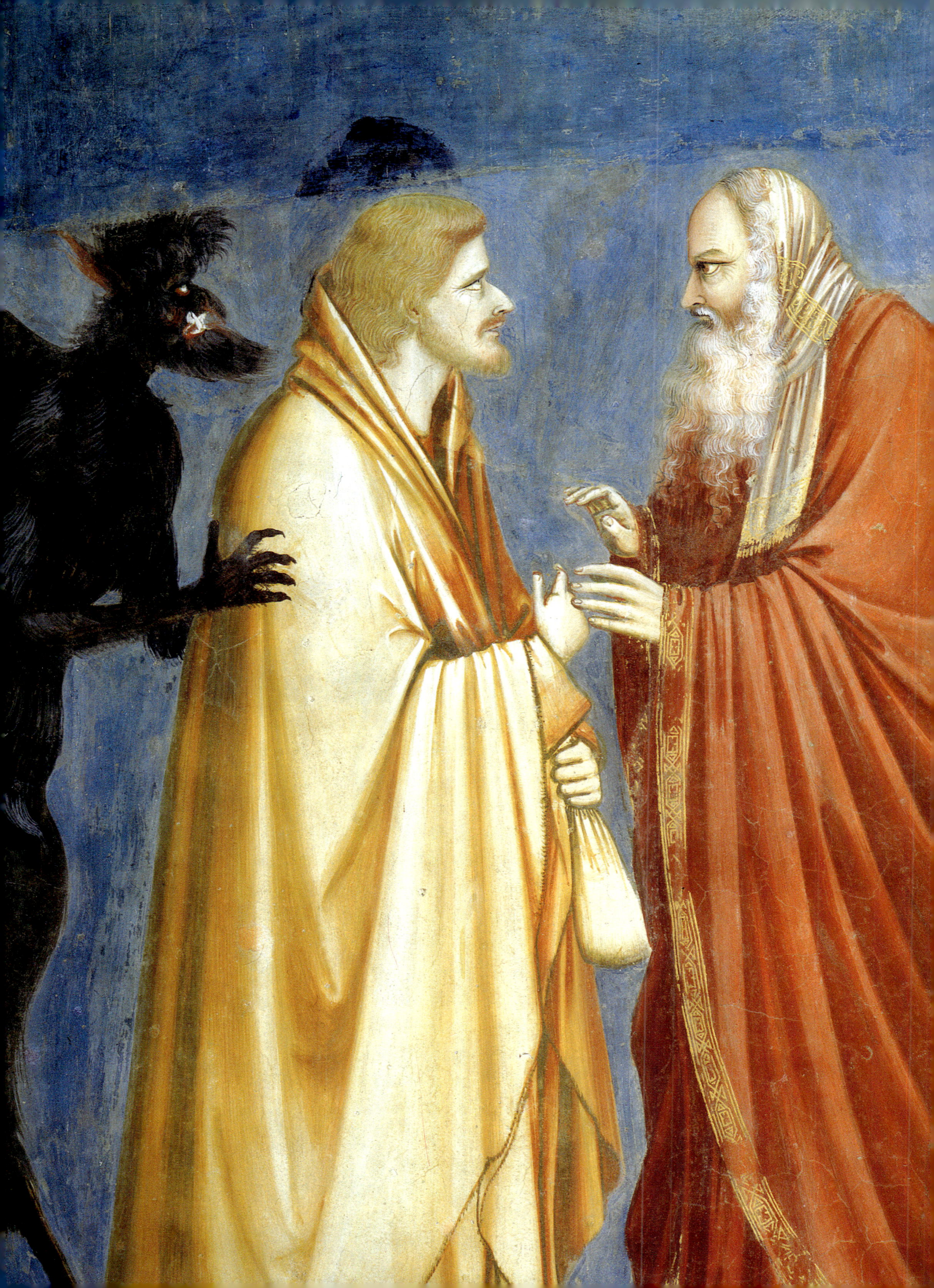

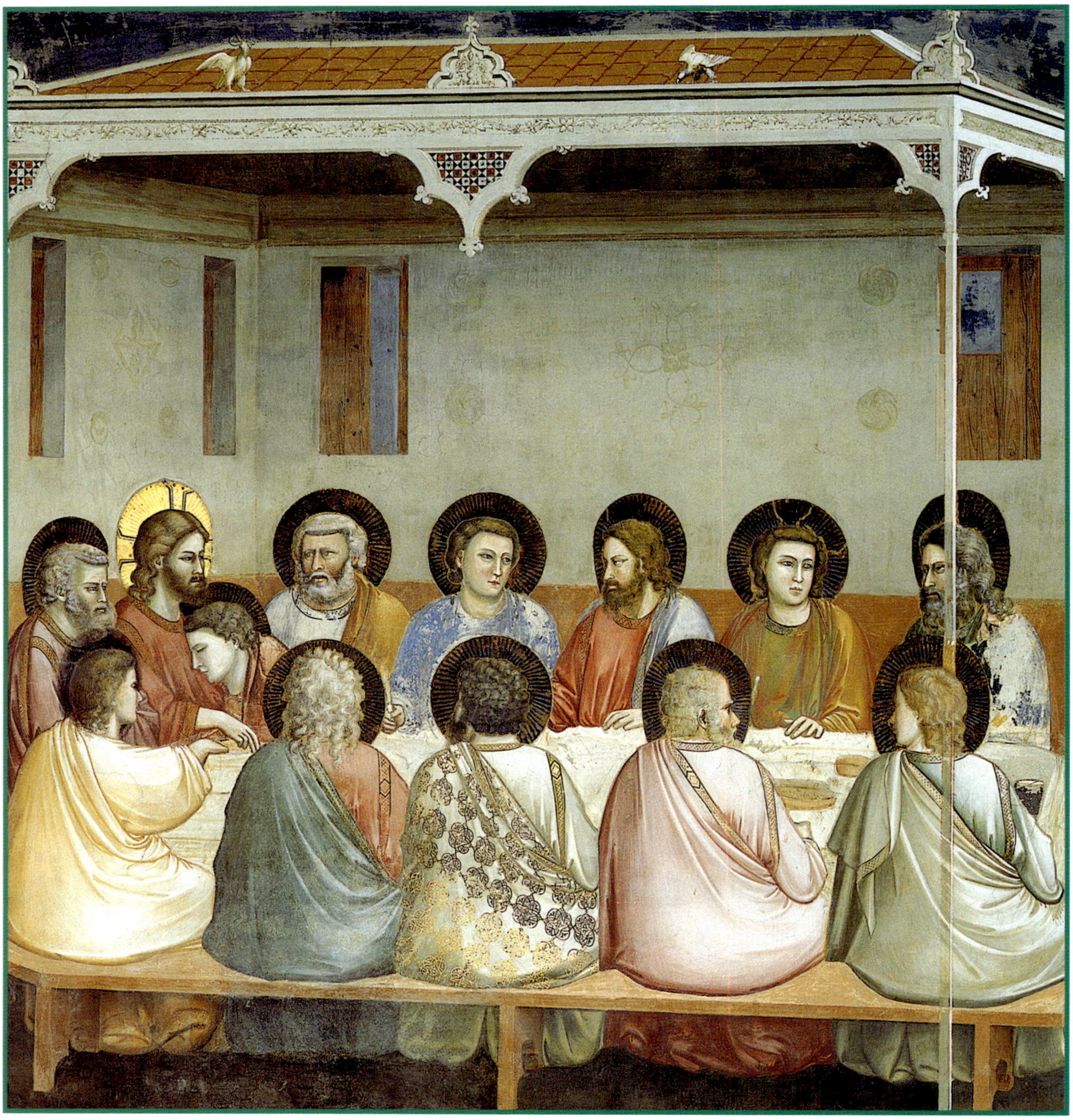

27. Last Supper
Once again we find Judas — in the refectory, during the last supper — stretching out his hand to dip a bit of food in the plate with Jesus. "One of you will betray me": Jesus' words seem to pierce the faces; each person asks himself who he is. Once again Giotto has painted the betrayer's halo black (those radiating from the other apostles, gilded with a mixture of copper, silver, gold and lead, have oxidized with time). Chosen together with the other eleven apostles, he, too, was offered a good destiny; instead, he followed the idol (money, a self-interested calculation about how tings were expected to proceed). And everything slipped down the slope of heavy "mel-ancolía" (black humor, melancholy), towards a consistency of evil and the most tragic and desperate final decision. He is contrasted by the infinite tenderness of John — "the disciple whom he loved" — with his head lying against the breast of the Friend. The two men's cloaks are the same color, and coincide even in the border designs. Love and charity: charity which remains in the present by way of the eucharist sacrifice, instituted during that last supper. This fresco recalls the nearby altar presided over by Giovanni Pisano's fine *Madonna and Child*.

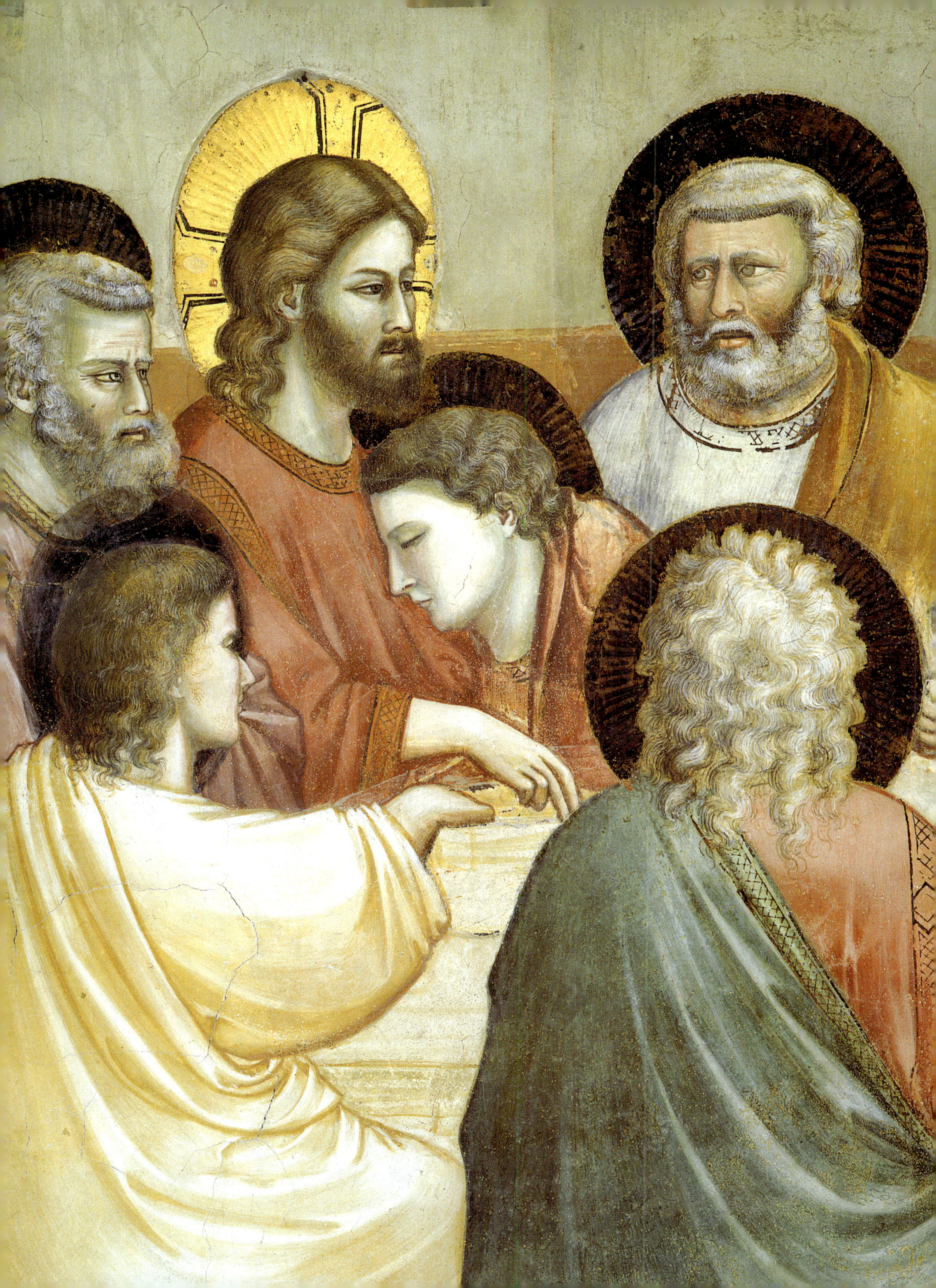

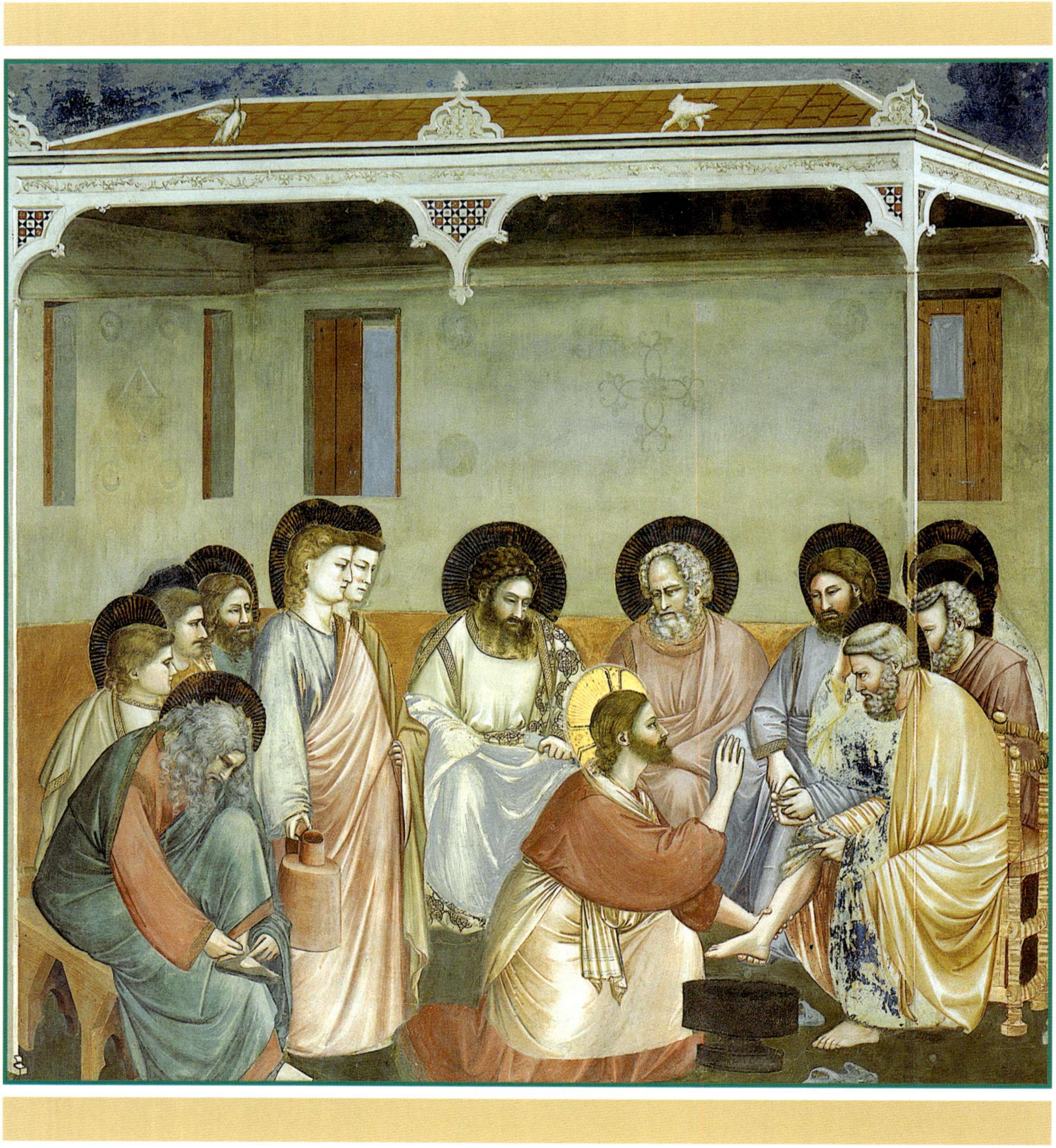

28. Washing of the feet

The place is the same: the refectory of the last supper, in fine oblique perspective, with the same windows; the figures are the same. Jesus kneels; bound by a towel, he is about to wash Peter's feet. With his left hand Peter uncovers his leg, while with his right he indicates that he is willing to have his head washed as well. Judas looks on in nervous embarrassment; John, who is standing, is holding the water jar. Like the first of the Magi in the upper part of the chapel who bows toward the Child, Jesus, the "Lord and Master", bends down to wash the feet of the Twelve. He thus gives an example, inviting the others to do the same among themselves. Peter, ardent as always, has first put up resistance, then exaggerated in the opposite direction. The exchange of glances between himself and Jesus is marvelous.

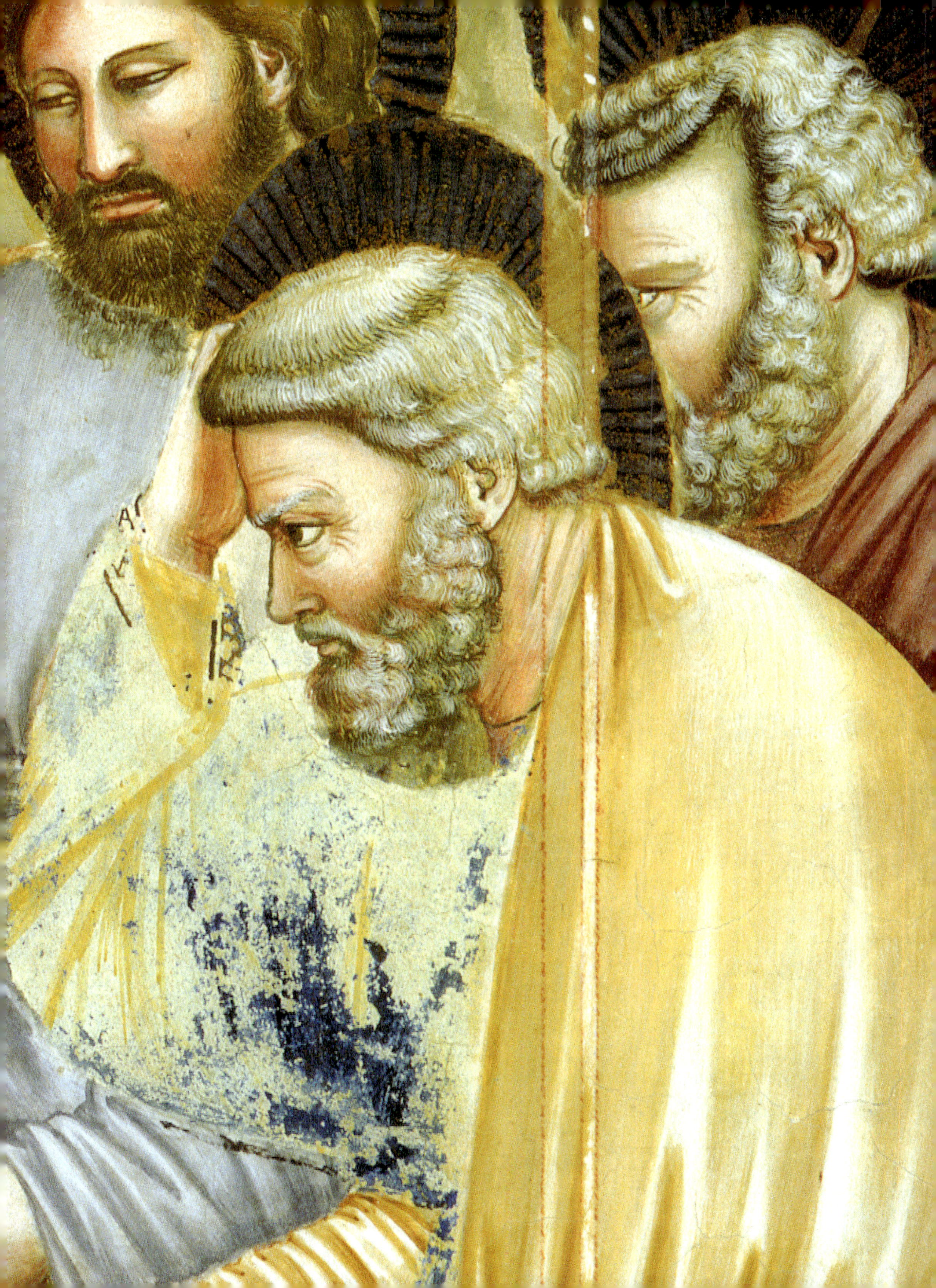

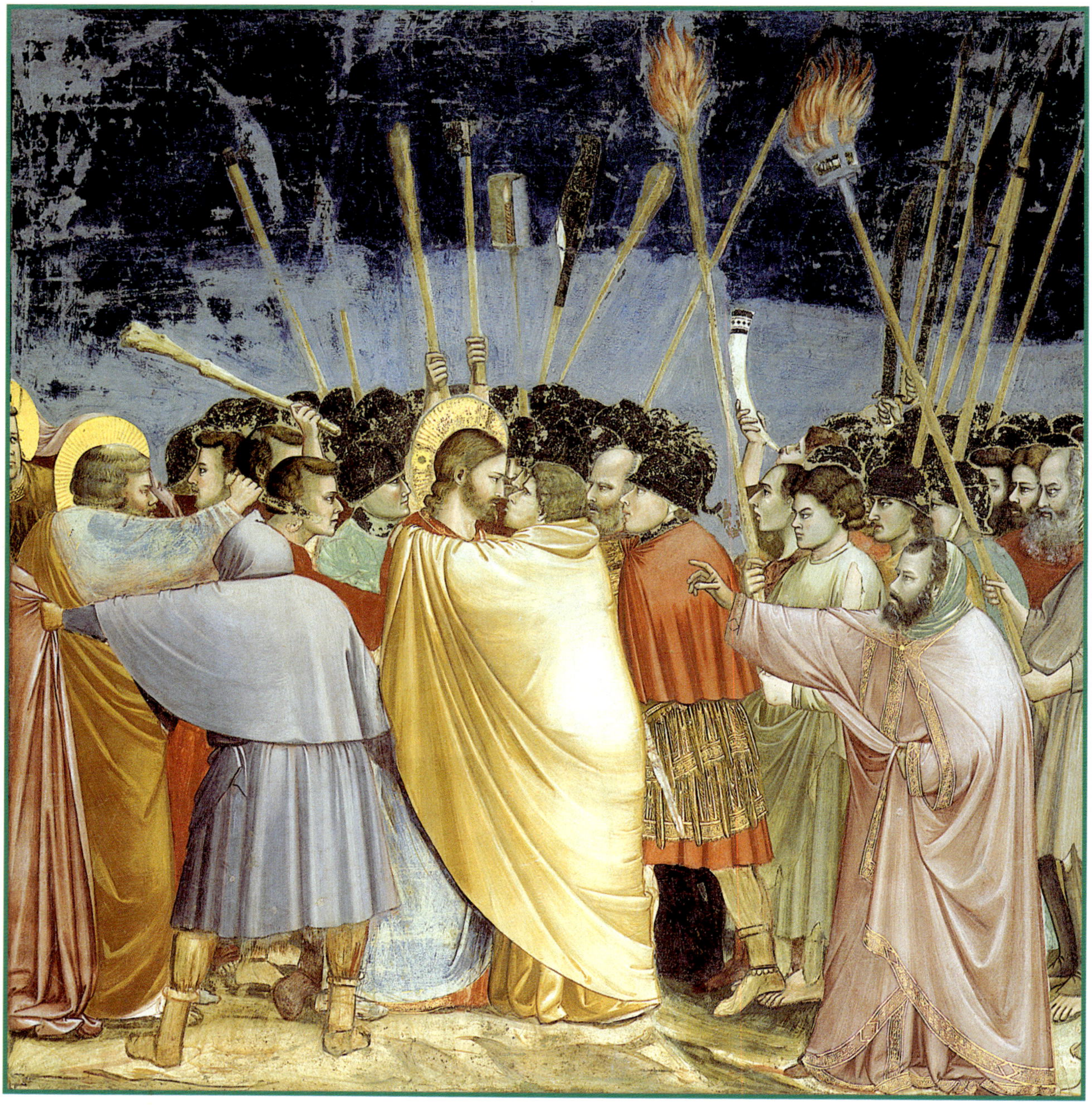

29. Kiss of Judas
Leading the soldiers, Judas reaches the olive orchard; he embraces Jesus, enwrapping him in his yellow cloak: this is the kiss of betrayal. The geometrical center of the picture is hidden, it is the heart of Judas, which Judas has entered (John 13:27). The window to that heart is his cutting glance toward Jesus, responded to by the divine tenderness of one who calls him back, even in that supreme moment: "Friend ...". Underneath a leaden sky against which stand out "lanterns, torches and arms", as well as a knotty club and a horn, the black helmets of the front group of soldiers form a murky frame in the center. Amid the general excitement (counterpointed by strong color contrasts), Christ stands unruffled.

On the left, as a thug shoves him violently, Peter is again carried away by his temper: he cuts off the ear of Malcus, the high priest's servant. In the right corner, the other pries t— the one wearing the red cloak, who had handed over the thirty silver pieces — scrutinizes the scene with an evil look.

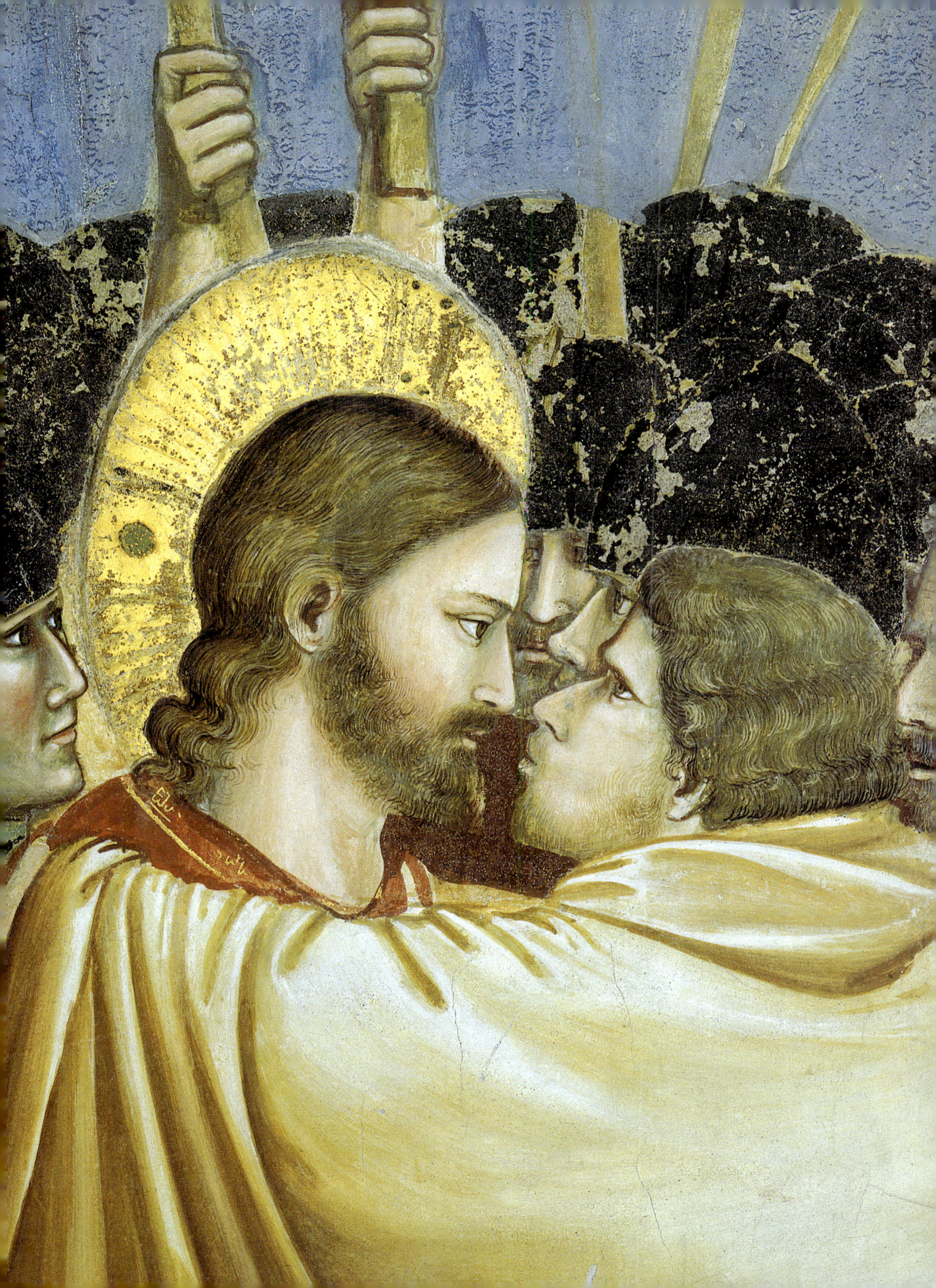

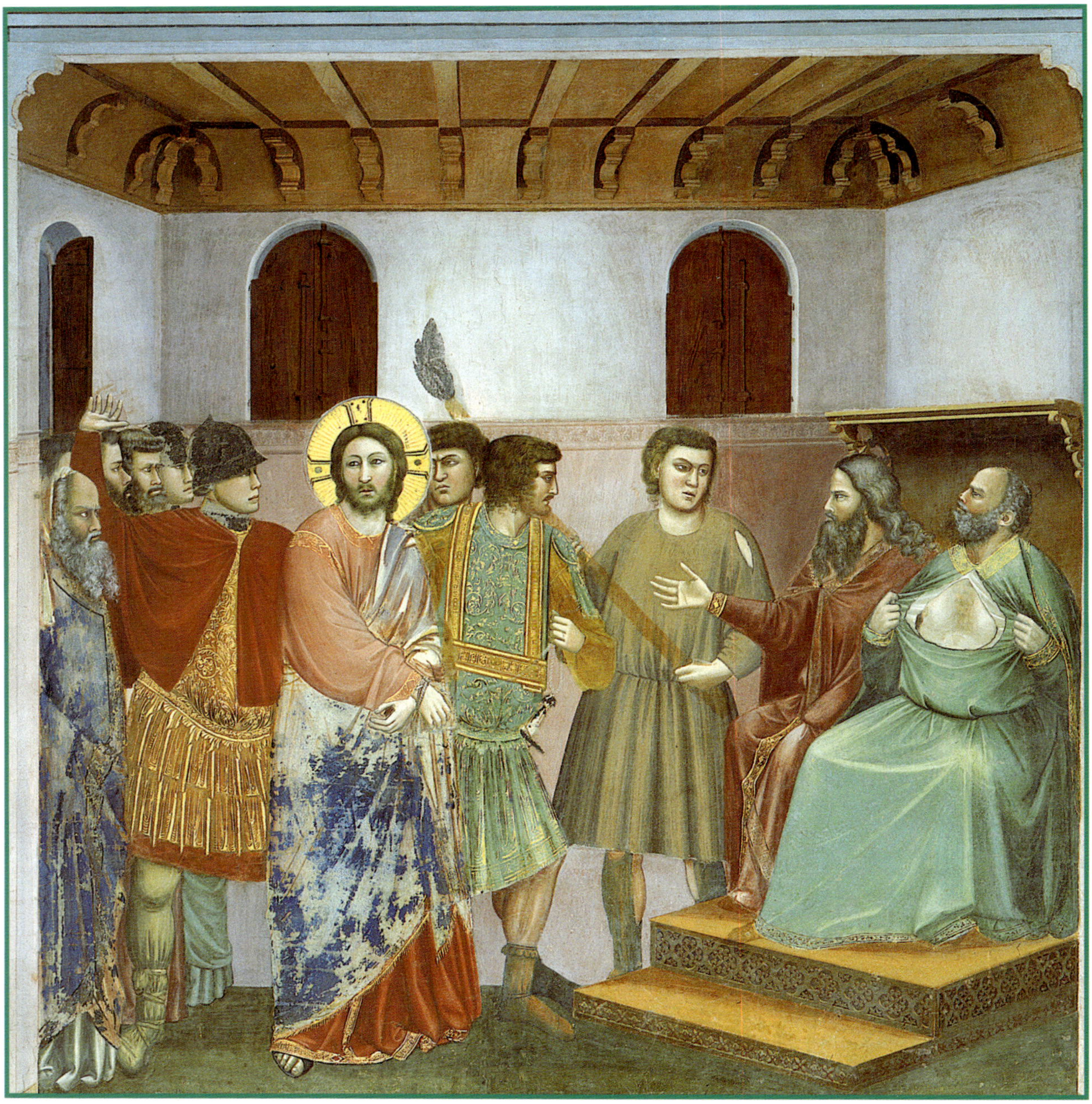

30. Jesus before Annas and Caiaphas

This series, which had opened in the evening with the two scenes set in the room of the last supper, closes symmetrically at night with two similar scenes, within two settings which are different, but marked by the same semi-frontal perspective: Jesus before religious power here, and before the civil and religious powers together, in the picture following.

Responding to a precise question, he comes to an explicit declaration: he is "the Messiah, the Son of God". Giotto represents the moment following this confession: wrathfully Caiaphas (recognizable in his greenish habits) rents his clothing in the presence of this "blasphemy". Annas sits at his side. A soldier raises his hand to slap Jesus, and he turns to look at him with the meekness of the innocent lamb which is about to be sacrificed. Fourth from the left, Peter hides among the little crowd, observing things.

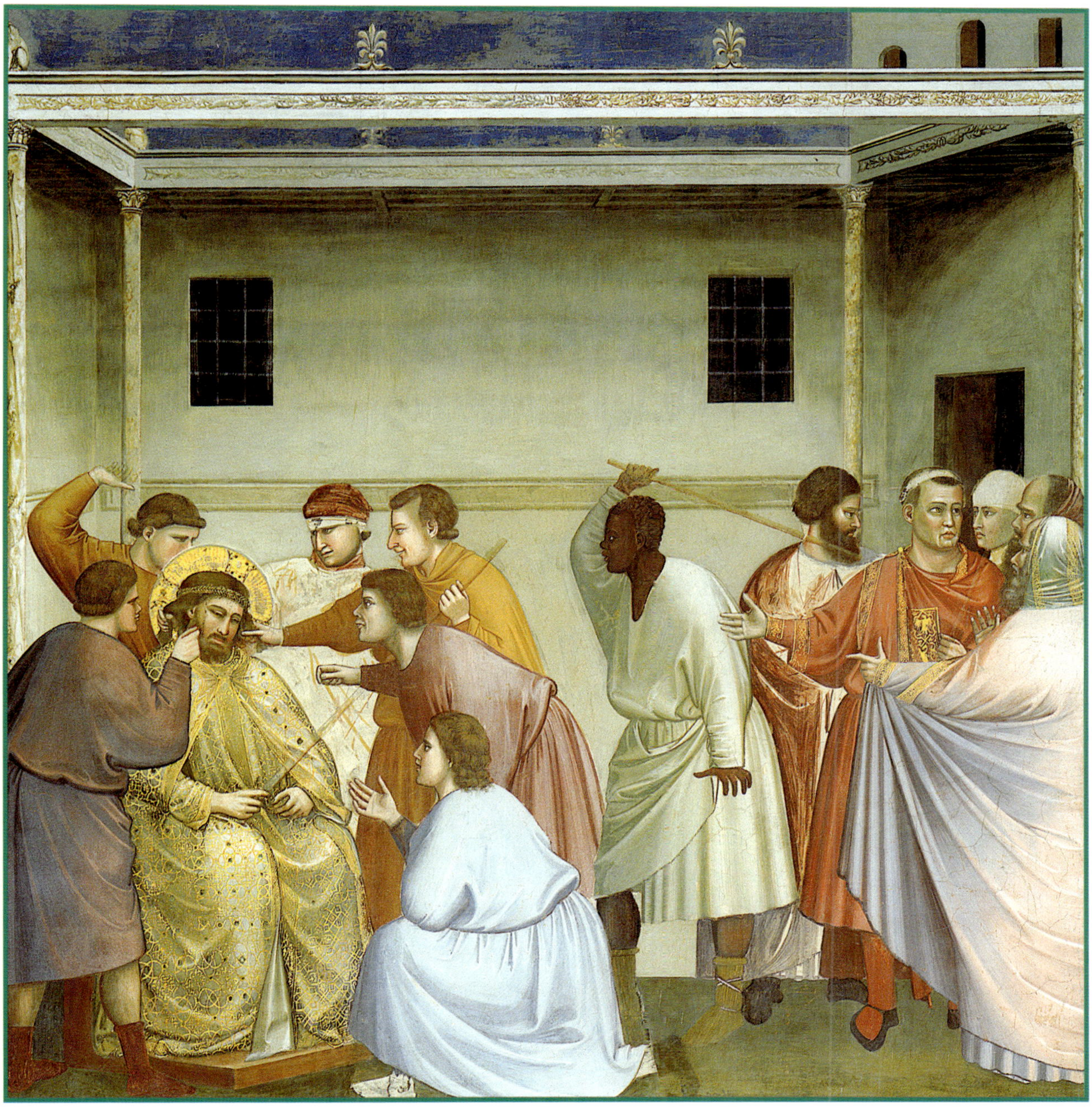

31. Christ ridiculed and whipped
Christ stands before Pilate. On the right, the governor wears a precious red cloak on which stands out a golden Roman eagle; at his back stands his wife; then, two priests talking to him.
Jesus is derided as "king of the Jews"; to ridicule him they have cloaked him in a golden royal cape, crowned him with thorns and given him a reed as scepter. Six thugs encircle him: one slaps him (in the identical position, the same gesture as in the preceding picture), one pulls his beard, one his hair, one kneels before him in mocking reverence. At his back a black is about to hit him with a rod. These ruffians are "characterized in detail" (Basile) as to psychological temperament.

The play of vertical correspondences is striking: in the upper area, Herod orders the slaughter of innocents; in the lower one, Christ — the innocent lamb — appears imprisoned in a room whose windows are barred, while the high priests and Pilate are about to fulfill the plan launched by Herod thirty-three years before.

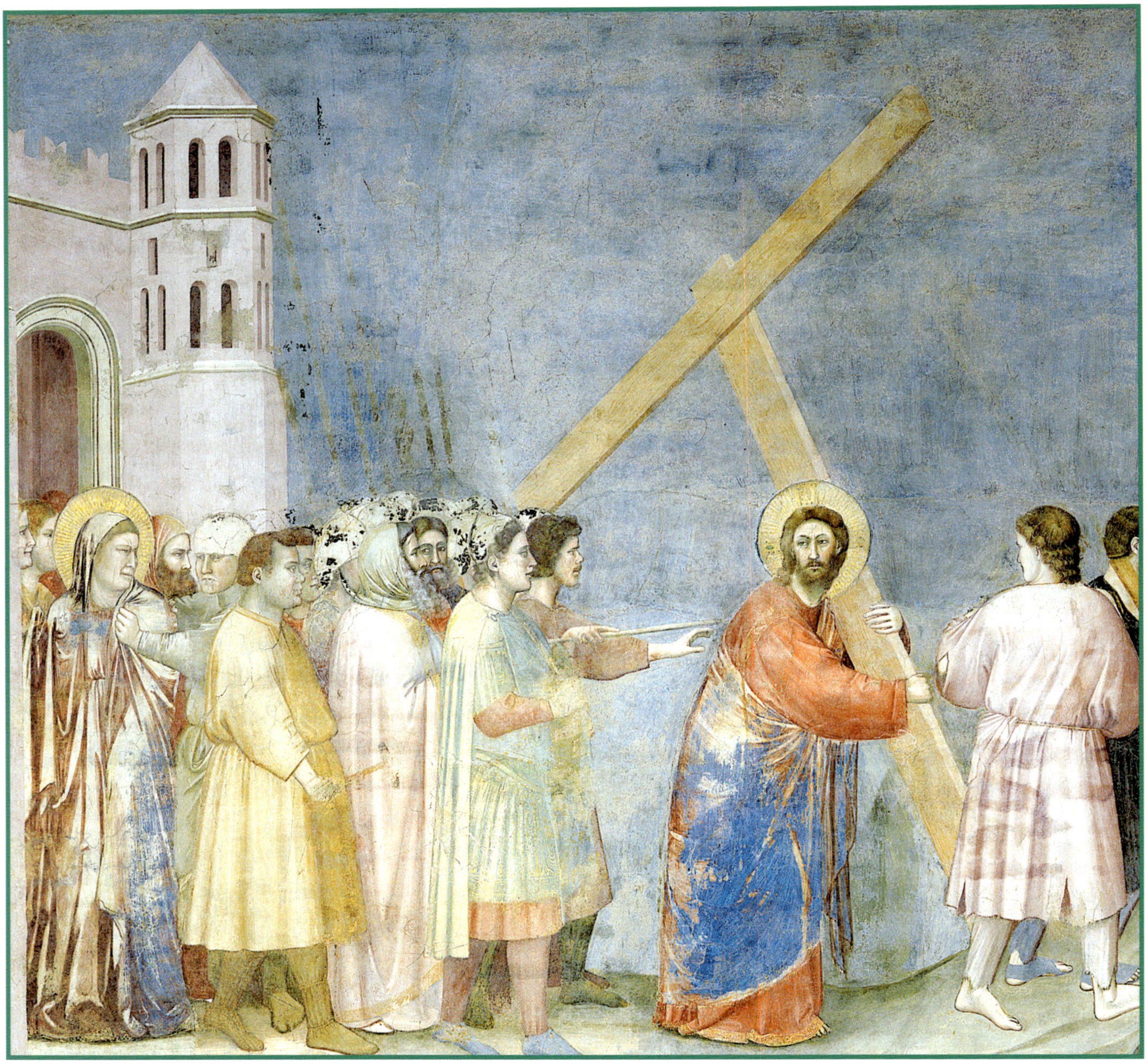

32. Jesus goes up to Calvary
The gates up high on the right, through which Jesus triumphantly entered Jerusalem on the back of a donkey, is the same one, down on the left, through which he now leaves, burdened with the cross. He seems to embrace that cross. Instead of palm fronds and olive branches, now it is spears which stand out in the sky, with a sinister air.
Before him, barefoot, is the man from Cyrene. Behind Jesus a soldier goads him with a stick. At the gate stands the mother, her face afflicted, shoved around by another soldier. He turns as if looking for her, with the same eloquent look of a meek, innocent lamb that he has there, in the front, when he is brought before Annas and Caiaphas: a silence which speaks, of one who, in the upper fresco, has instructed the rabbis in the temple.

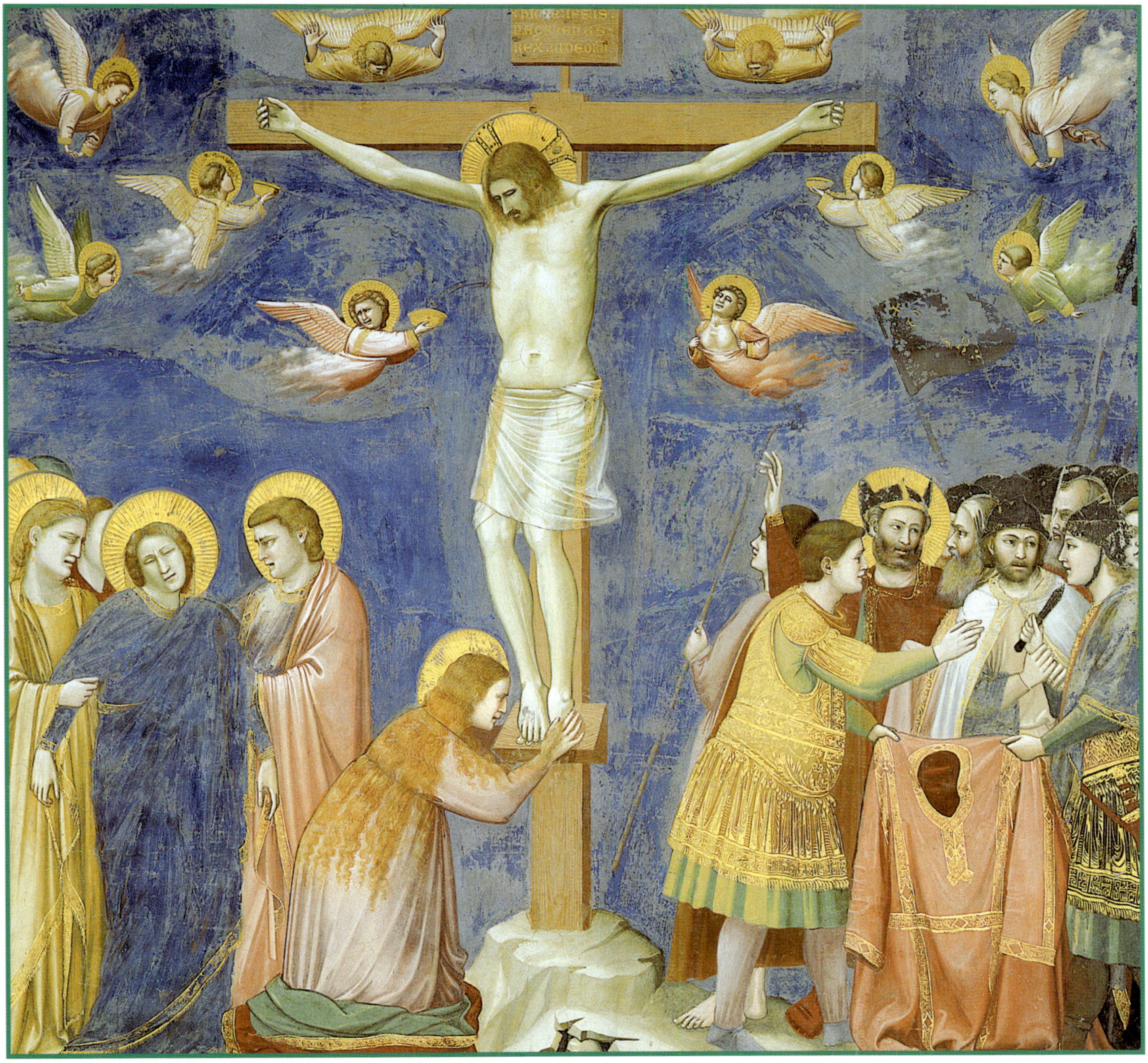

33. Crucifixion

From the cross Jesus seems to embrace us. He is surrounded by the grief of ten little angels, the same that we had seen in exultation above the Nativity hut. Three of them hold up a chalice (the grail) in which they collect the blood form the nailed hands and the pierced side. Pain, in heaven and on earth. On Jesus' right, John and the first of the three Marys sustain the Mater dolorosa, so shaken that she is about to faint. Lapis lazuli blue completely enwraps her: here is the kind embrace of the Mystery, crossing through such lacerating circumstances. On the other side, to the left, the flag of Rome, with its "S.P.Q.R.", can be seen faintly above the soldiers, who are about to gamble with dice for the seamless red tunic. This is the supreme apex of God's love. In the group, wearing a halo, the centurion points him out: "Truly, this man was just" (Luke 23:47). Right and left, the good and the evil; but among these last is one who recognizes and acclaims him: no Manichaean dualism here, no fatalistic predestinction, but always the freedom to betray (the kiss of Judas, there facing us) and freedom to recognize and change (like that of the centurion). At Jesus' feet, Magdalene: the woman that he had freed of the seven demons, now wipes away the blood with a lock of her long blond hair. At the foot of the cross is the skull: Golgotha, but also the ancient Adam, sprinkled with the blood of the New Adam. Death is redeemed.

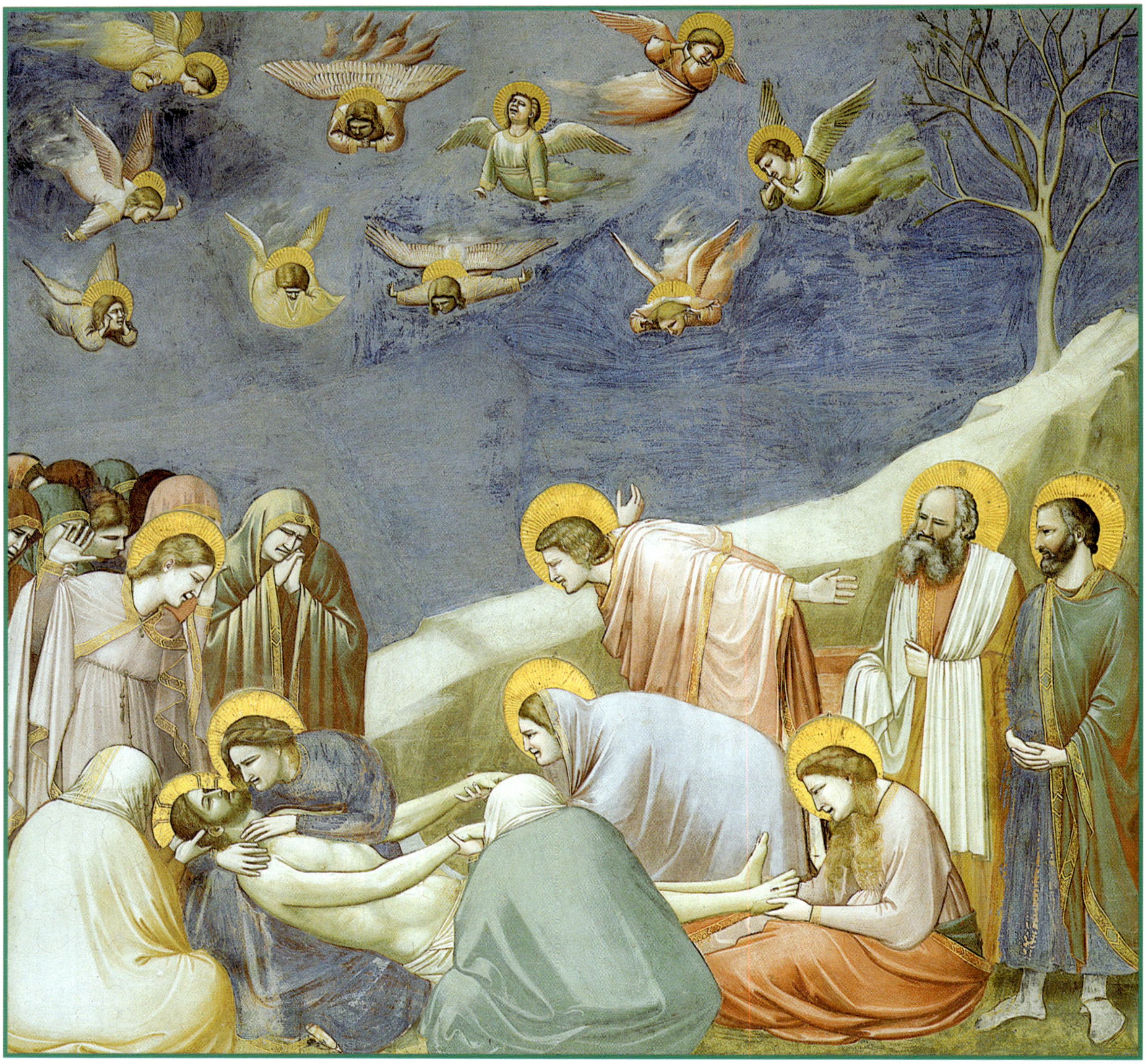

34. Mourning over the dead Christ

The infinite pain of the *Crucifixion* spreads to the *Mourning*. Grief of the angels in heaven, and of all earthly reality: from the withered tree up in the corner to the bare edge of the cliff, which seems to make our glance slip down to the mother's grief-stricken embrace. Carved into her face is immense pain, but not desperation: this is the specular image of the women who in the Nativity embraced the child in swaddling clothes, with a calm face, though already veiled with sadness (for "the life of man is made up of joy and pain in equal parts").

In the center, right at the cross point of the diagonals, the face of john, the friend who — throwing out his arms disconsolately — gazes at the Friend. Two men stand behind him in stone-like stillness, like two sculptures seeming plastically to explode outside the picture, and at the same time, to draw into it the pain of us, who stand before it: God is dead. On the far right calmly stand Nicodemus and Joseph of Arimathea, wearing like a stole that white winding-sheet in which the son will be bound, as his mother watches. Between himself and John we can make out the tomb.

An absolute masterpiece, given, as well, the "equilibrium created by the rhythmic alternation of empty and full spaces, by the bending or absorbed figures, by the color tonalities, in their delicate play of symmetrical counterpoint" (Giulia Sponza).

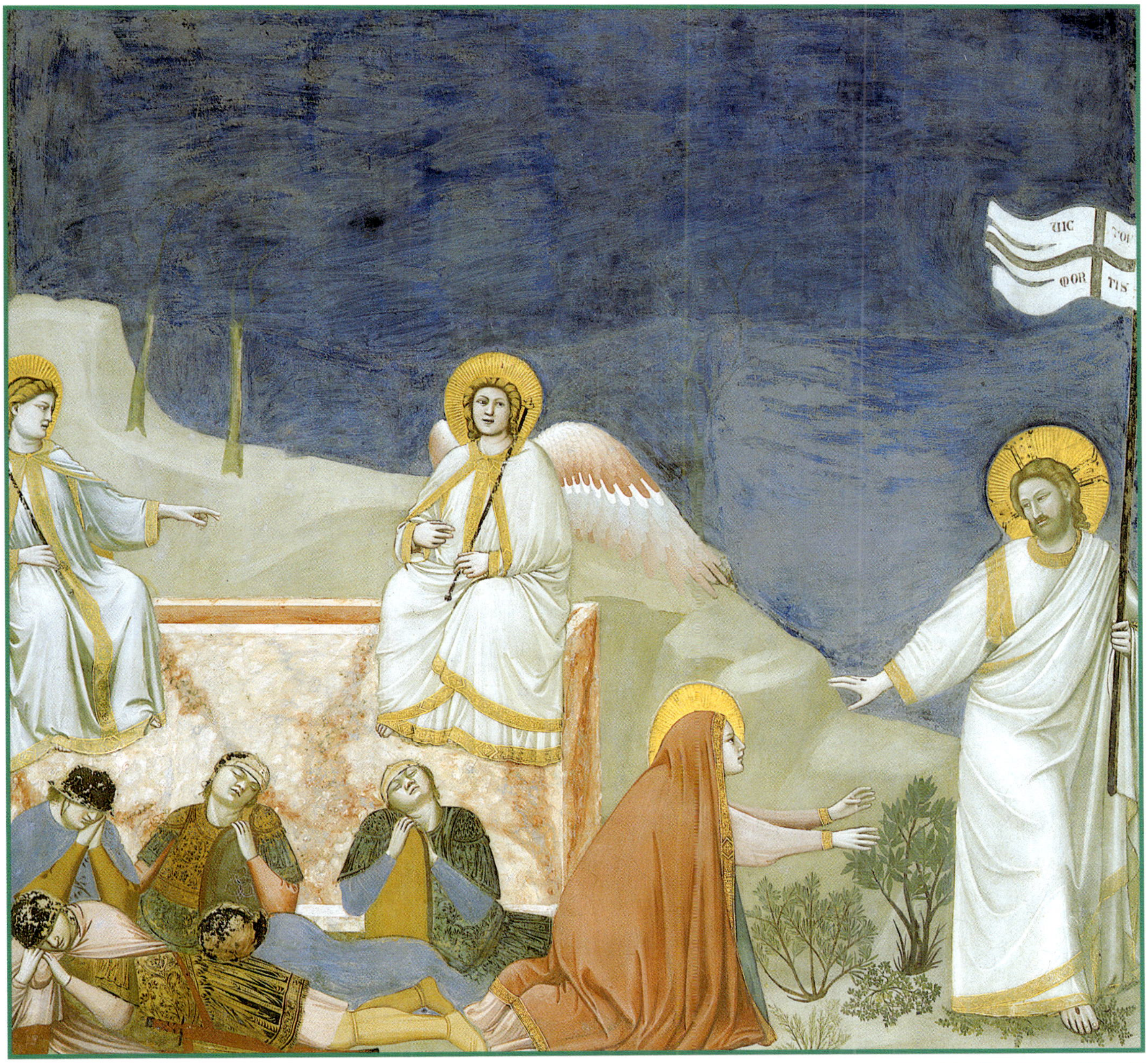

35. Resurrection

At the pink marble tomb sit two angels (see John 20:13-17); the one seen in profile is pointing to Jesus, while the other, facing us, is holding the thin scepter of victory, topped by a cloverleaf motif.

The ridge of the cliff, which in *Mourning* had led our gaze leftward, now symmetrically guides us to the right: towards the radiant faces of Jesus and Magdalene, towards the gesture of those two outstretched hands, and of that other — time-honored focal center of the painting: *noli me tangere* — toward that foot which is already walking toward the Beyond. This is the ikon of felicity: "there are the two hands of Magdalene thus thrown forward, and the hand of Christ which marks the borderline. This is a threshold: the threshold is the end of a pathway and the beginning of another way of traveling. [...] Felicity directly understood, is the presentiment of happiness, it is prophecy. For on one hand, felicity is the fruit, the end of a path well traveled, the threshold of the home; on the other hand, felicity is the prophecy of a dwelling where not only will life be different, but where life will take over in all its splendor" (L. Giussani).

Three times over, Magdalene seems to "dwell" at the feet of Jesus: beneath the cross; in the successive *Mourning over the dead Christ*; and again, while kneeling, reaching out toward the Resurrected, who says to her: do not touch me. This is the vertex of the Magdalene triptych: possession with detachment, virginal possession. The red cloak

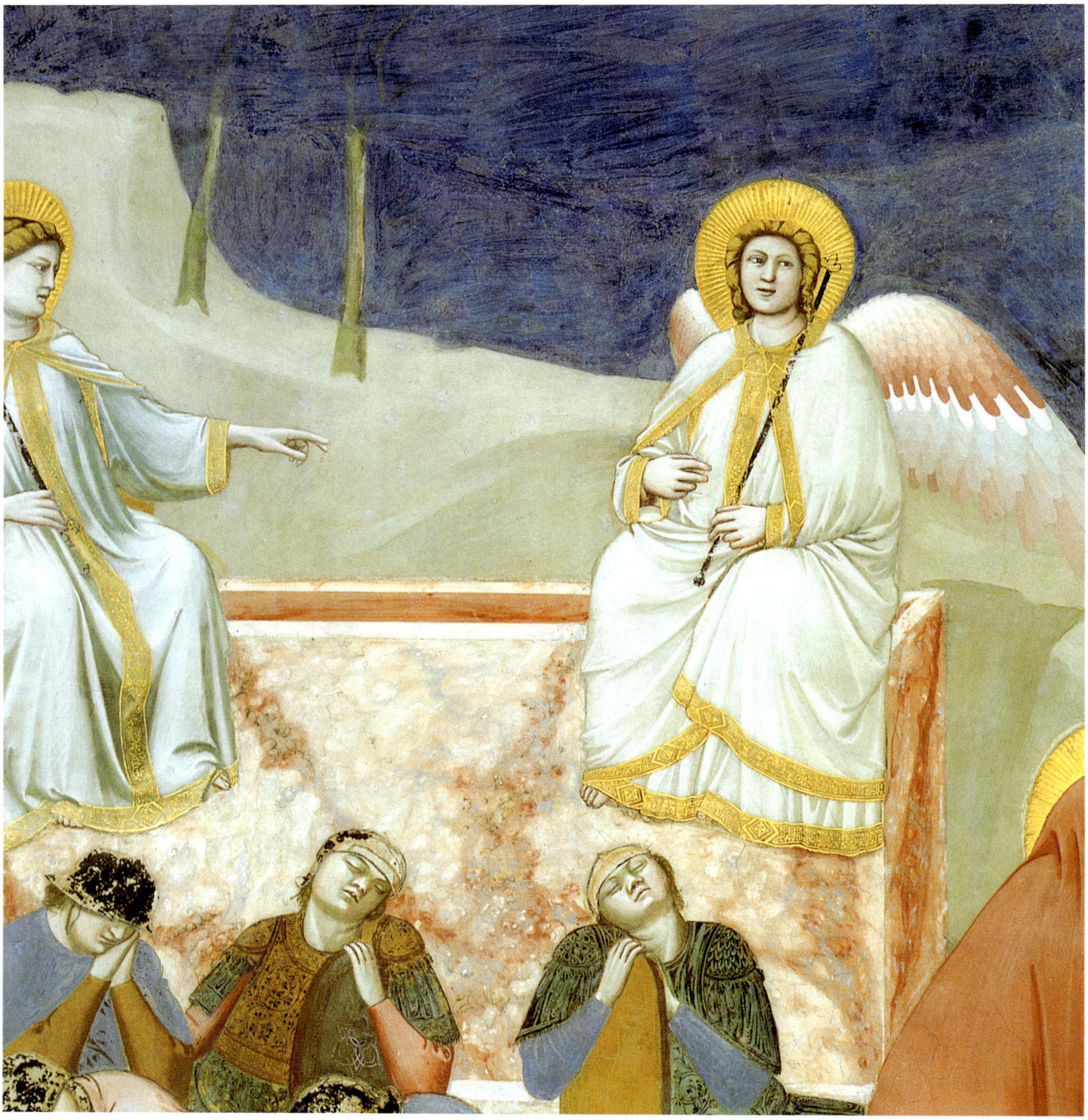

— love of charity — first underneath her knees, in *Crucifixion*, and which partially covers her in *Mourning*, now totally enwraps her in *Resurrection*. A short distance away there is only the dwelling of awaited felicity.
The Resurrected holds up a banner with a white cross motif, on which two words stand out, ten letters in all (three for each four paintings: the symbology of numbers!): "VIC-TOR MOR-TIS", Conqueror over death. The Gospel — the most sweet news — is here, in these twelve letters that the Twelve will take to the ends of the earth. And the earth, arid the day before; now flowers again, bright with greenery: we see two trees high on the right (though a repainting has covered their foliage), and tender little bushes, and soft grass beneath the wounded feet of Jesus. The open-mouthed, wide-eyed dromedary in *Epiphany* signals the animal world; here is the vegetable world: everything participates in the various moments of the Event.
But this is not so obvious in man, in whom human liberty is at stake: as in the picture directly above — the spring *Resurrection of Lazarus* — there are some who, despite the power of fact, will go to denounce Jesus to the Pharisees; these will then decide in favor of his death. Similarly, in *Resurrection* we see on the left that group of soldiers sleeping, who will say shortly: "his disciples came in the night and stole him away, while we were sleeping" (Matthew 28:13). A glaring lie, destined to be short-lived: if you were sleeping, how can you say this? In order to

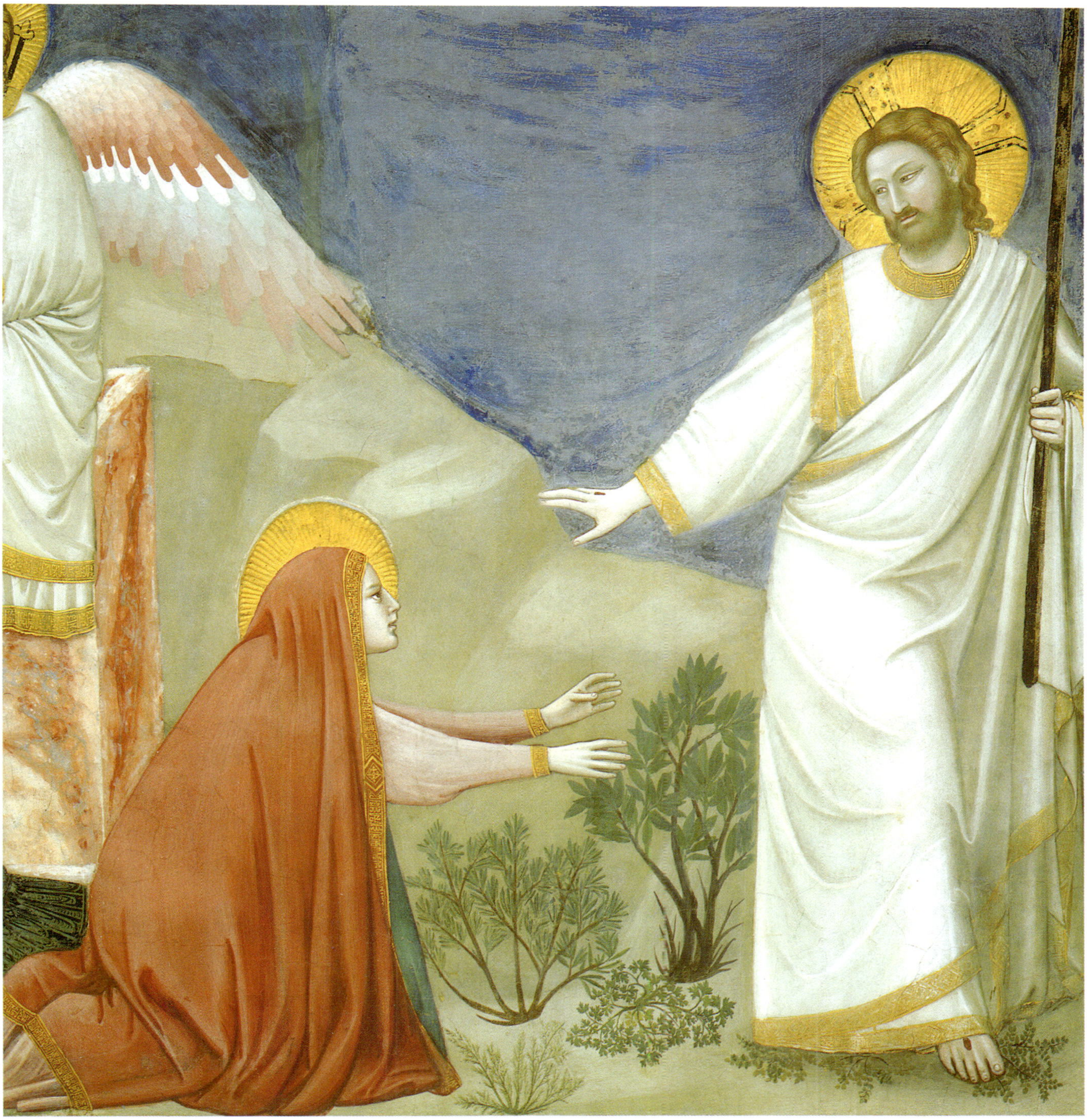

unmask the devil — the father of lies — and his soldiers, logic is sufficient. And against an overcast sky, the Truth emerges more resplendent than ever: he has risen.

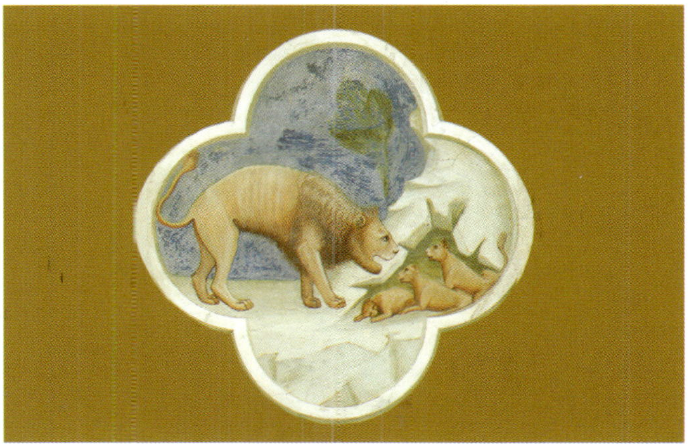

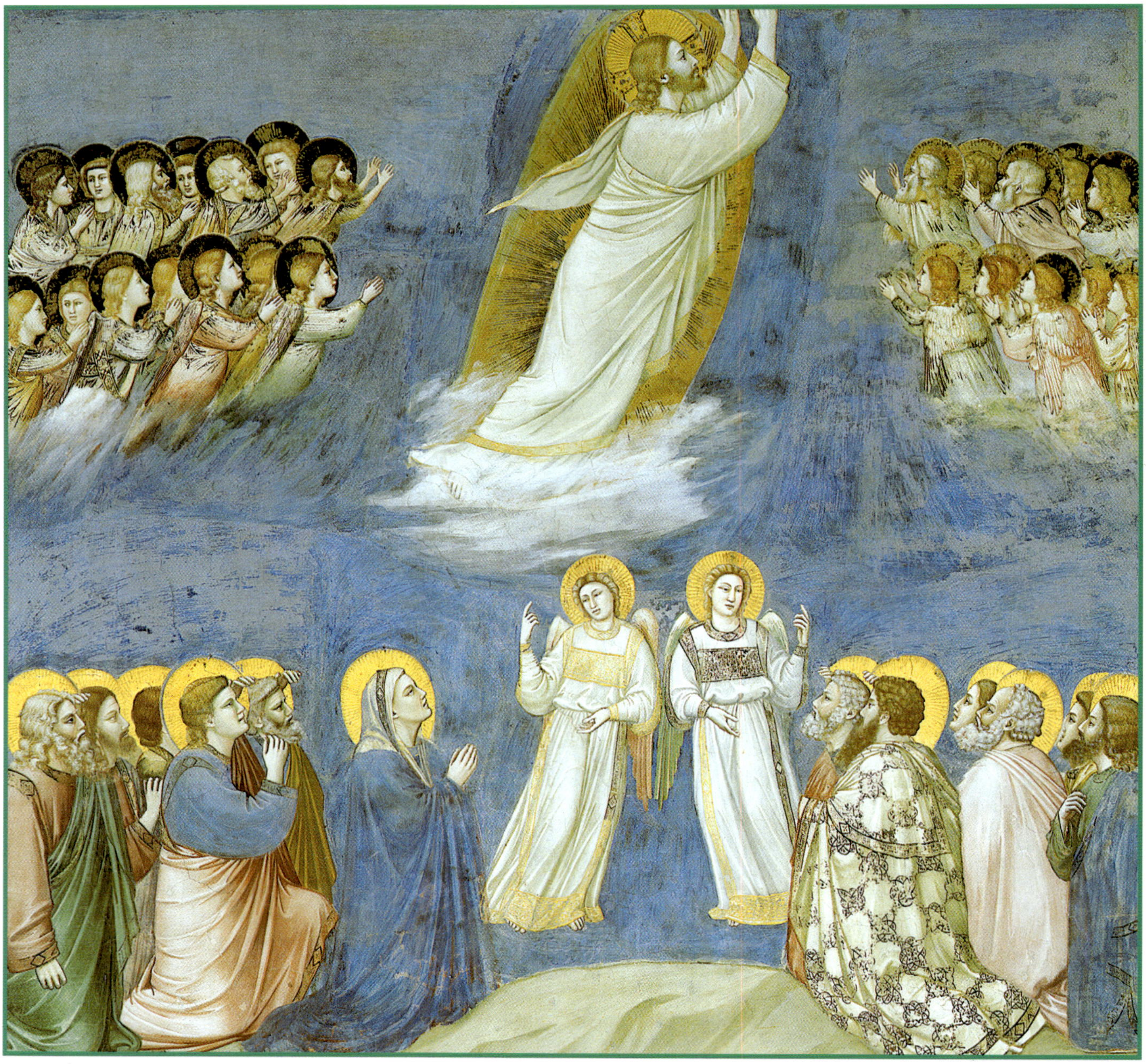

36. Ascension
As the forty days of Lent had precede the Holy Week, the apex of the divine redeeming enterprise, so forty more days follow the Resurrection before Jesus ascends to heaven; or rather — since for ancient men, height and depth correspond — before he descends into the farthest depths of all things; his hands seem to sink into them.
He stands out resplendently in the golden mandorla (maternal threshold of the Beyond), above a pure white cloud. He is surround, as if twice crowned, by twelve saints reaching out toward him (the first on the left is John the Baptist), drawn into heaven with himself after he descended into Hell; and twelve winged. From the earth as well, the bodies and glances of twelve figures rise toward him: form left to right, Andrew, James, Judas Thaddeus, John, Peter and Mary; then Matthew, Bartholomew, Thomas, Simon, James son of Alphaeus and Philip. The rich cloak stands out marking the presence of Bartholomew, as it does in *Last Supper* and *Washing of the feet* and, on the side, in *Pentecost*: two on the right, two on the left, we find the four pictures with their clear portrayal of the apostles, they will reappear in *Final Judgment*.
In *Ascension* everything flows from the sides toward the center, from the lower region toward that point, high up on the right — at the top of the triumphal arch — where sits the throne of the Father. Two splendid angels levitate over the little hill (see Acts 1:9-11); with a specularly sym-

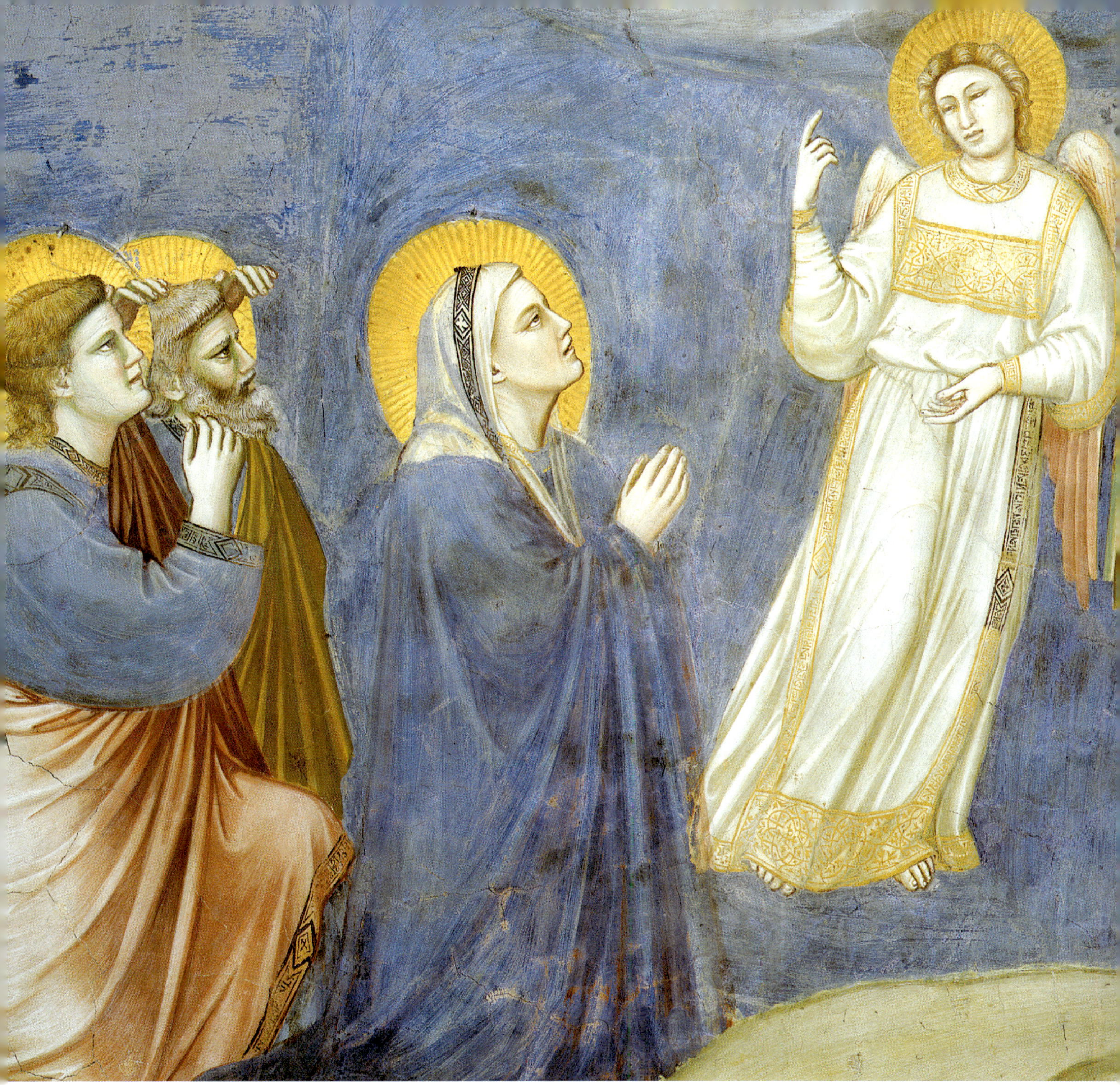

metrical gesture appear figures which are "ponti-fex", serving as bridges between earth and heaven. With one hand they welcome the militant Church, and with the other indicate the triumphant Church. Up front, Mary, slightly detached from the group, is completely dressed in the blue of Mystery. She contemplates the glory of the son, her face ecstatic, her forehead wrinkled, her mouth half-open. Hers is a joy faintly dimmed by a veil of sadness. The same sadness makes itself felt, behind her, in the faces of Peter and John, who with their lift hand protect their eyes in order to see till the last moment, the radiant friend who is leaving them. Everything here — gazes, gestures, colors, refined embroidery on the garments, in heaven and on earth — expresses the calm exultation of saintly joy: Jesus "the conqueror over sin and death, has preceded us to the eternal dwelling, in order to give us the serene hope that where he is, our leader and the first-born, we, the members of his body, shall be as well, united in the same glory" (first preface to the liturgy of the Ascension).

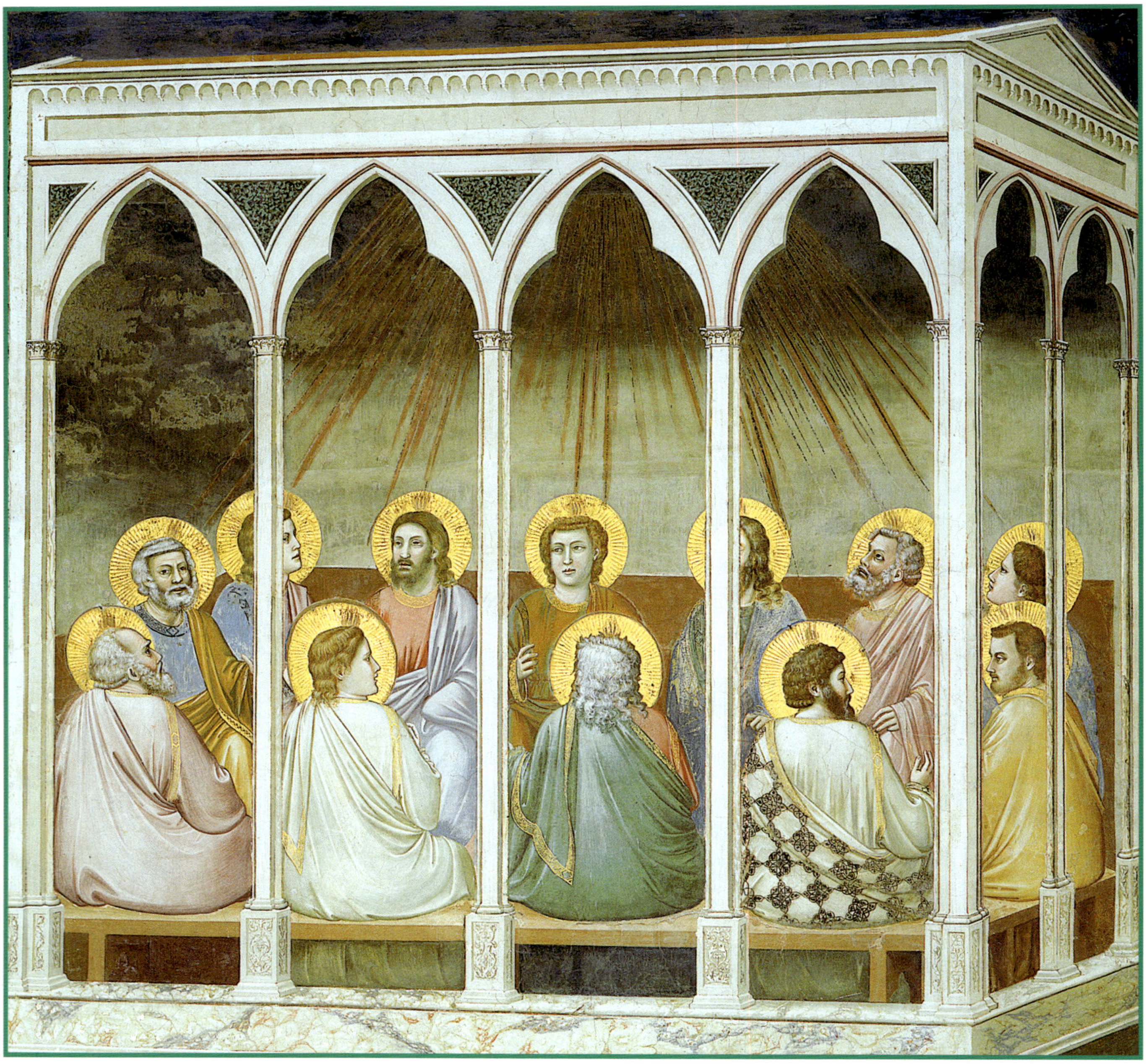

37. Pentecost

Pentecost: that is, the fiftieth day after Easter: the descent of the Holy Spirit (see Acts 2: 1-11). The Twelve—the Eleven of Ascension, joined by Matthias (sitting on Peter's left) in place of Judas — are gathered together in the room of the Last Supper, when "there appeared to them tongues as of fire; these separated and came to rest on the head of each of them. They were all filled with the Holy Spirit" (Acts 2:3-4). Giotto sets this passage on stage, faithful to the letter. Christ, who has ascended to the heaven of the Mystery, from there — from a spring which "breaks through" the painting — irradiates his Spirit, which now shines redly, against the gold of halo, above each person's head. The circularity of communion is the source of faith's radiance; in different languages it will spread to concentric circles, till it reaches the ends of the earth. Painted light rains down; real light breaks in through the windows of the opposite wall, through painted Gothic windows. By way of Peter's eyes, which stare us in the eye from the left, the light of the Spirit comes out and reaches us in the real world; and — right at the closure of the cycle of the redeeming Event — confers on us the task giving value to our lives: to announce that Fact. A "most delicate architectural modulation" (Bellinati) marks the room of the Last Supper — that is, the newborn, resplendent Church — which appears as a circumscribed, well-defined place: this is the emblem of belonging, as the source of true openness.

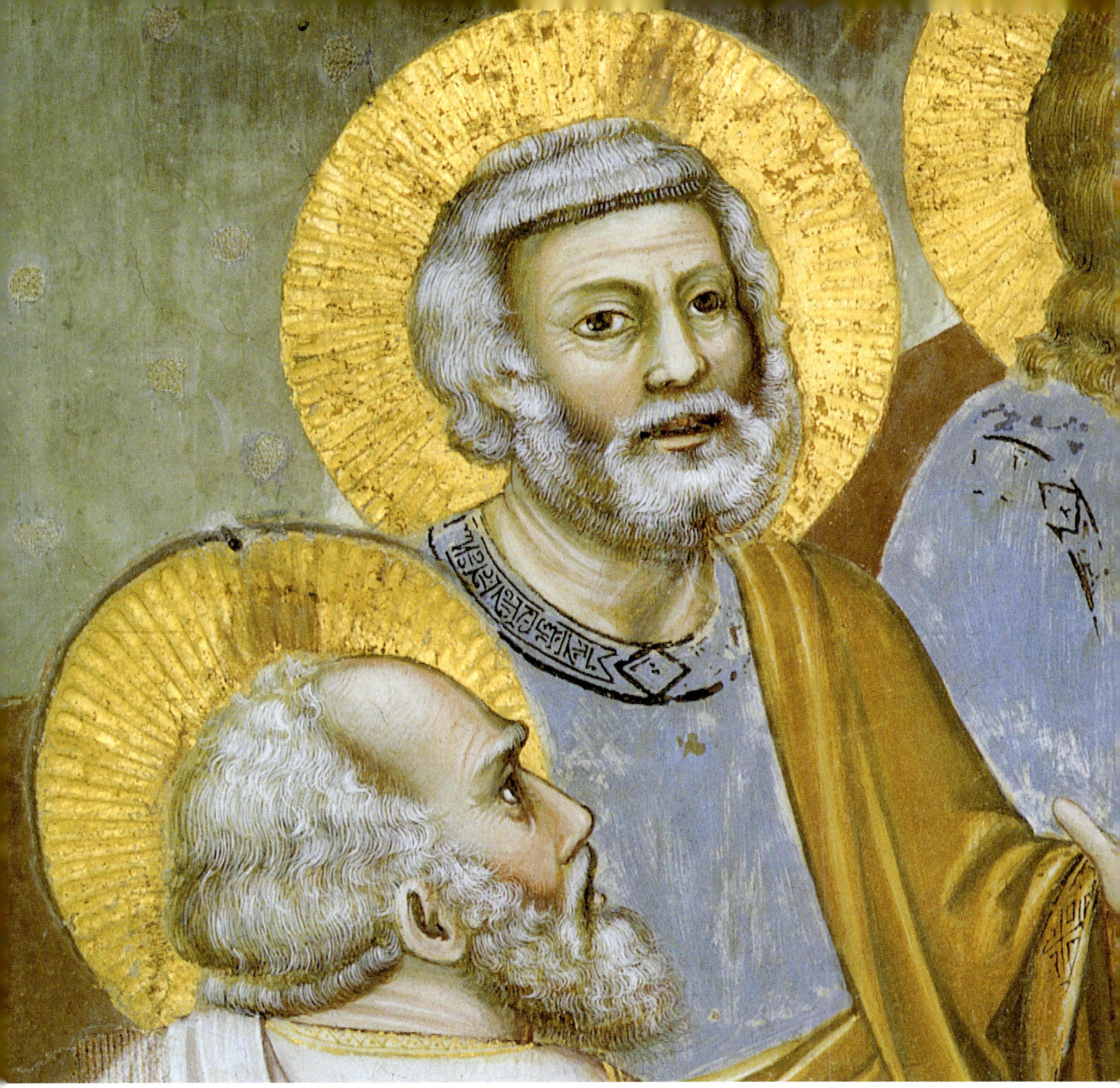

Here, and on p. 53, are two of the ten four-lobed tiles set between one picture and the next, on the north wall: ten emblematic episodes of the Old Testament which prophesy the same number of events in the life of Jesus, as painted in Giotto's frescoes. A symphony of "all the details, all of then, excluding none".

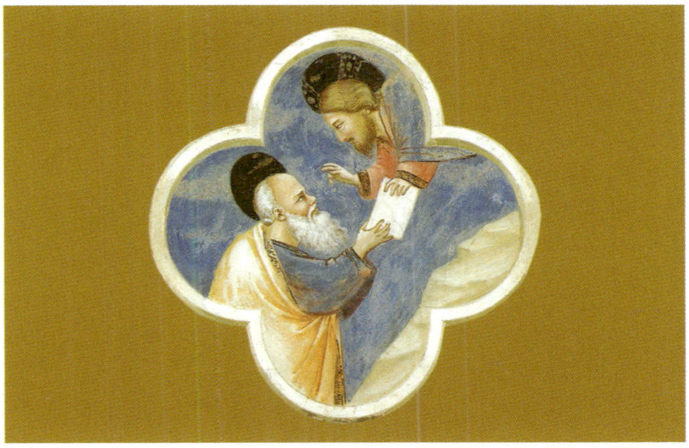

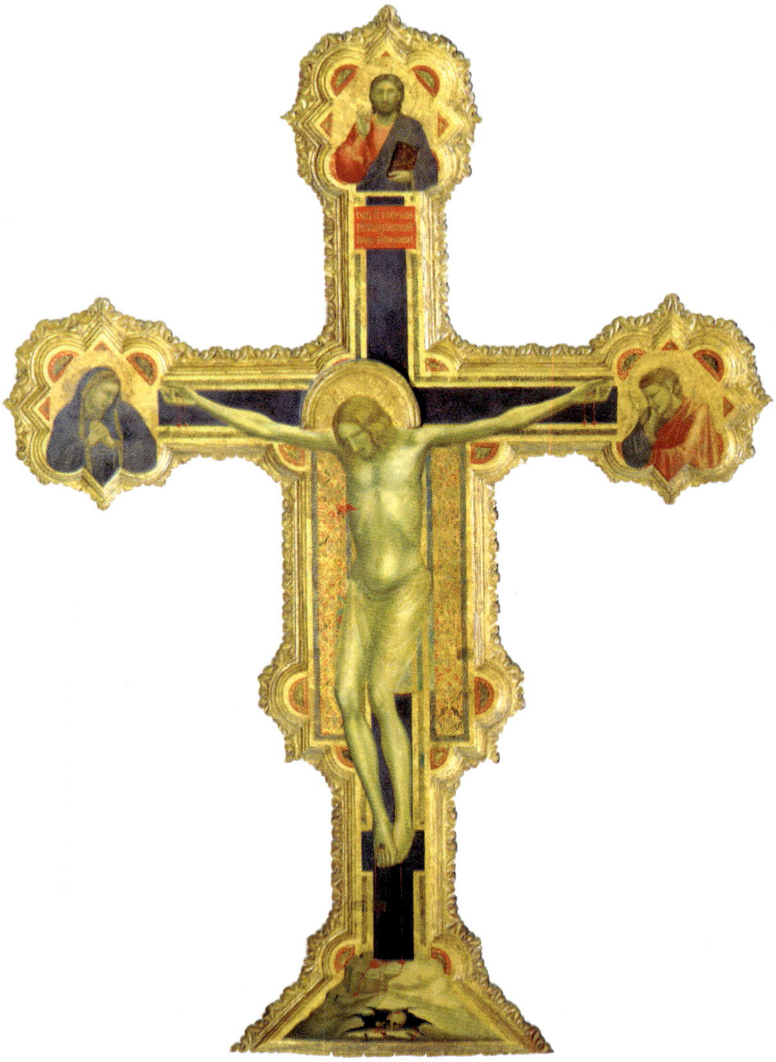

38. Crucifixion
The body of Jesus stands out against an elegant framework, against the background of a most refined Oriental fabric — a lampasso — even more precious than the one decorating the altar of the temple (on the right, *Presentation of Jesus;* on the left, *Consignment of the twigs and Flowering*). When this wooden *crucifix* (now in the Museum) stood in the Chapel at the center of the iconostasis, the faithful visitor could glance at it from many spots, from the corner of his eye. The wood of the Cross is the altar on which He is immolated, the innocent Lamb (painted behind, in the center; at the ends are the symbols of the four evangelists: the Word has make itself flesh, crucified and resurrected flesh).
The vertical arm represents the death of the New Man who, in the dynamics of descent, has come down from heaven and given his life, in order to sprinkle with his own blood the old Man; the skull of Adam, thrust into a grotto and reached by a red trickle at the foot of the Cross; and Golgotha means "skull". In the dynamics of ascent it represents human death assumed by the death of God, and saved (for this reason, "sister death"); and then projected towards the destiny of glory: Christ triumphant, with one hand raised in blessing (three fingers united: the Trinity; the other tow crossed: divine and human nature in the same person); in the other hand, the Bible; that is, the Word which is He himself.
On the horizontal axis, as he seems to embrace those who walk toward him, with a gesture of the hand, Jesus seems also to say to the Afflicted Woman: "Woman, here is your son", and to the disciple that he loved: "Son, here is your Mother". An embryonic Church springs up.
One more detail. On the scroll, two short words precede the canonical phrase (in acrostics INRI): "Hic est Ihesus nazarenus rex iudeorum". Those two words, "hic est" — here is — were introduced into the iconography of the Cross by Giotto's teacher: Cimabue. The disciple who — as Dante says — superseded him, thus pays homage to him in "code". It is by following the Master that one becomes truly great!

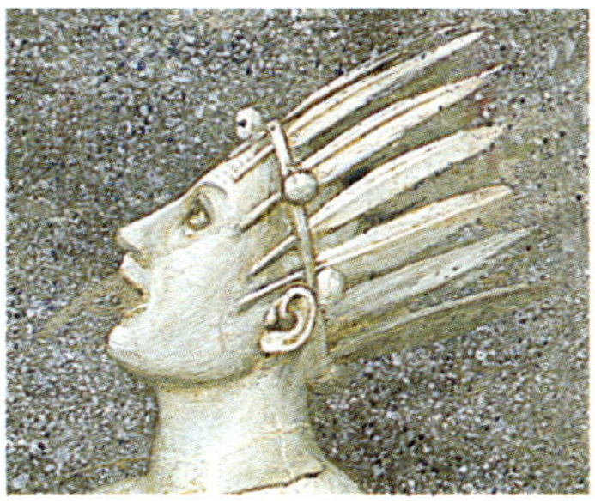

STOLTEZZA

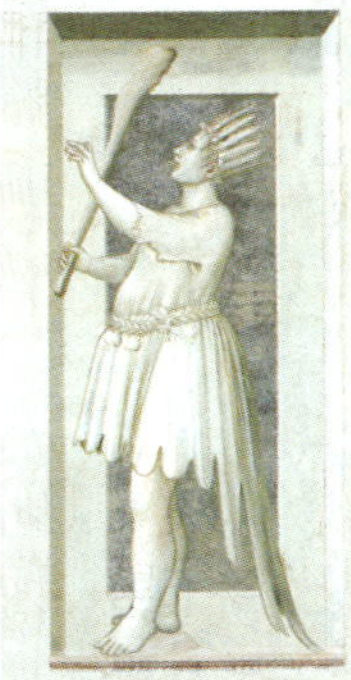

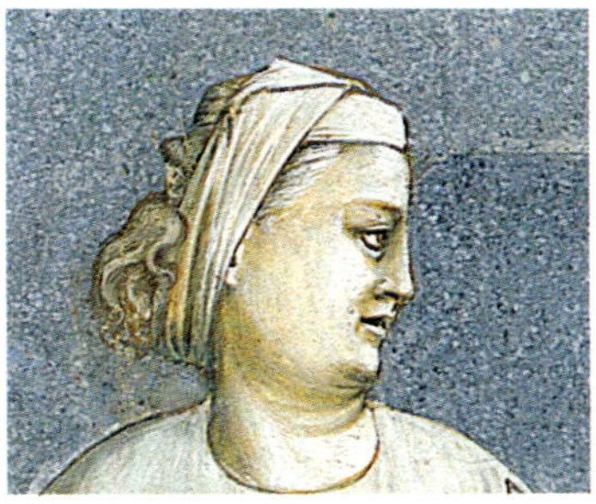

PRUDENZA

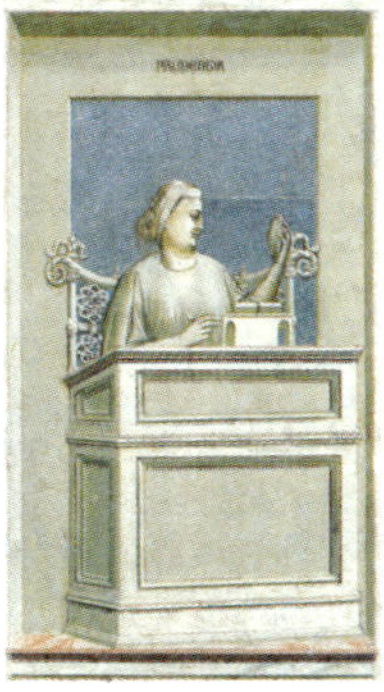

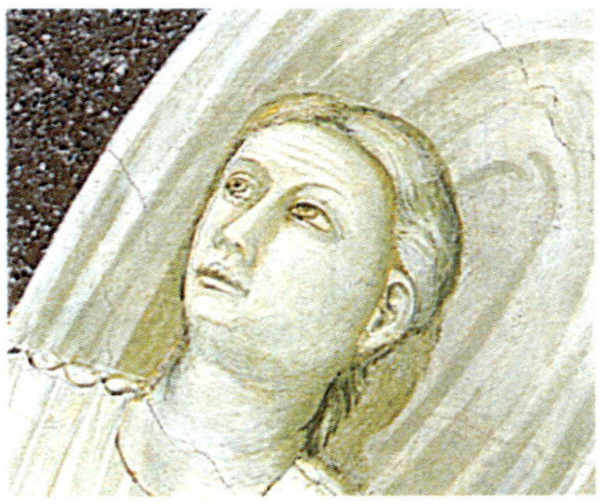

INCOSTANZA

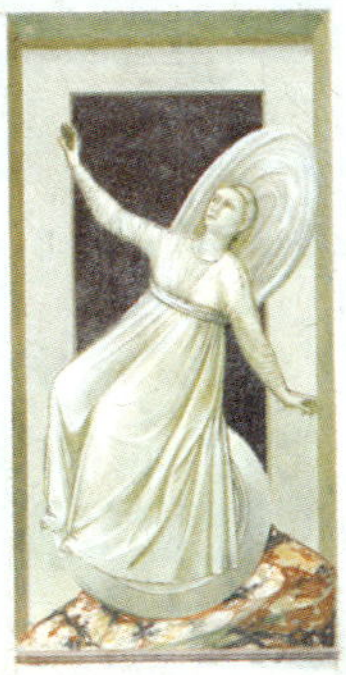

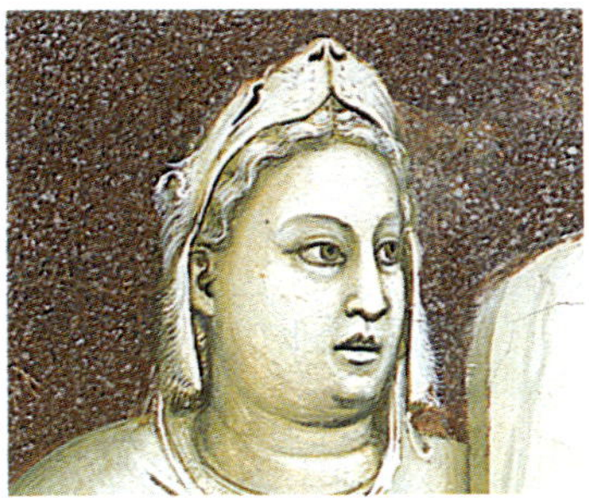

FORTEZZA

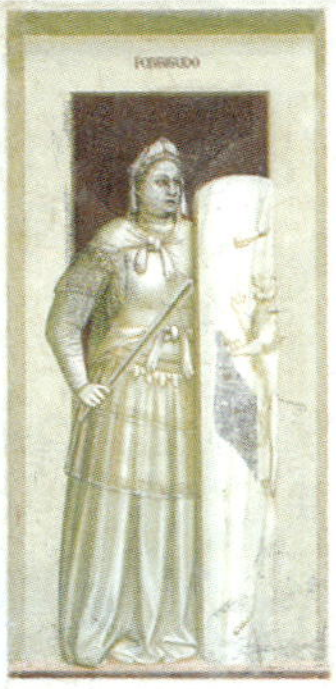

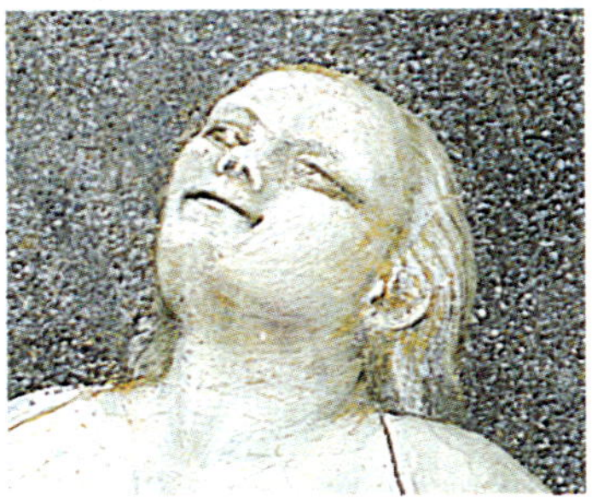

IRA

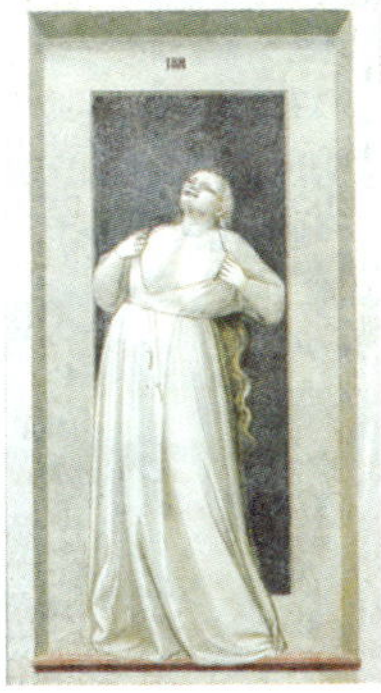

39. Vices and virtues

In the three upper frescoed areas Giotto has narrated the Event, that story lasting around fifty years: from the Immaculate Conception of Mary to the Pentecost. That Event which cuts history in two: before and after Christ. This area, the lowest one, presents the moral consequences of that Event: the personifications of the seven vices and the seven opposing virtues, four cardinal and three theological. Here is the attraction of Good and disgust for Evil. Not in full color, but monochrome: for color connotes the fascination of Christ from which it descends; though in the dimness, not by individual effort but by superabundance of the heart. The vices lead to Hell, over which, in *Final Judgment*, on the opposite wall, Christ the Judge closes his left hand. The virtues lead to Paradise, over which he opens his right hand. We see the seven pairs as we proceed from the altar towards the exit: all bear a Latin title, in highly lyrical notation, though often illegible now.

I.A: STULTITIA: a physically heavy individual, though he is "light" on the inside, inconsistent, fatuous, with his head in the clouds. With feathers on his head, the same that cover his body, and his left hand miming an ostrich head: everything in him evokes birds. And what is he hunting, with that club? Perhaps other birds like himself?

I.B: PRUDENTIA: this is the virtue of the teacher. He sits at the desk before a book. In one hand he holds a compass, and in the other, a mirror: he looks prudently behind himself, learning from tradition. But that mirror tells us something else as well: *speculum*, philosophical speculation, reflection.

II.A: INCONSTANTIA: in precarious equilibrium on a wheel running downward, she is falling back, as suggested even by her flying cloak: she is at the mercy of volubility and passion.

II.B: FORTITUDO: erect, determined, the right hand brandishing a club, in her left hand she holds up a large shield on which stand out a cross and a lion rampant. A lion skin forms her cape: the head of the beast is a helmet, the anterior paws are knotted at the neck, the posterior ones at the waist. Strong as a lion.

III.A: IRA: she rents her clothing, like Caiaphas, in rage over Jesus' "blasphemy" (and, in a play of antithesis, like the little angel beneath the left arm of the crucified Jesus: uncontainable pain, not wrath!).

III.B: TEMPERANTIA: her sword is tied up, and her mount is kept in check by a bridle: the tongue kills more than the sword.

IV.A: INIUSTICIA: a tyrant with claws on his hands sits on a throne, armed, in front of the ruined gate to a castle (or city), with Ghibelline merlons. The landscape facing him is wild, while the road is infested with bandits who kill, rob, rape.

IV.B: IUSTICIA: she sits regally on a Gothic throne, facing the city gates. She holds up a scale on which she "weighs all things with great fairness", as we read in the inscrip-

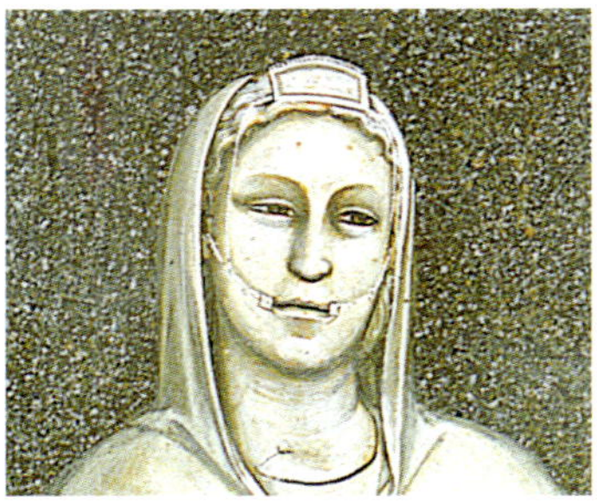

TEMPERANZA

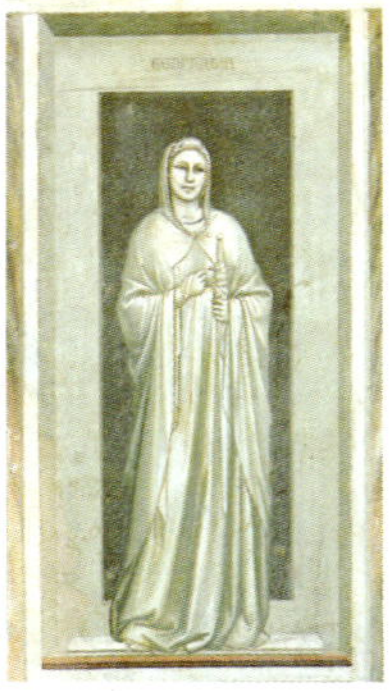

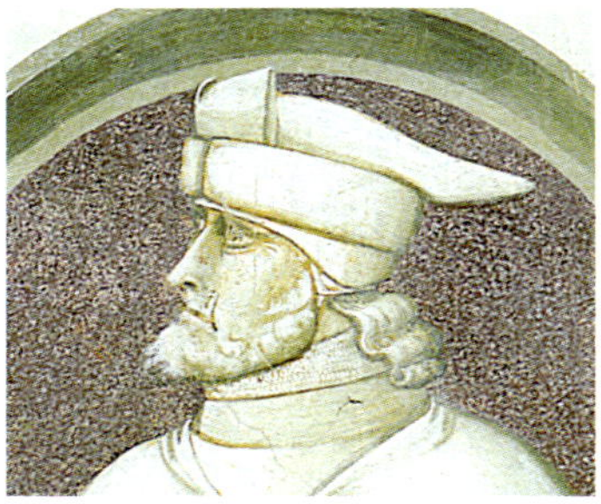

INGIUSTIZIA

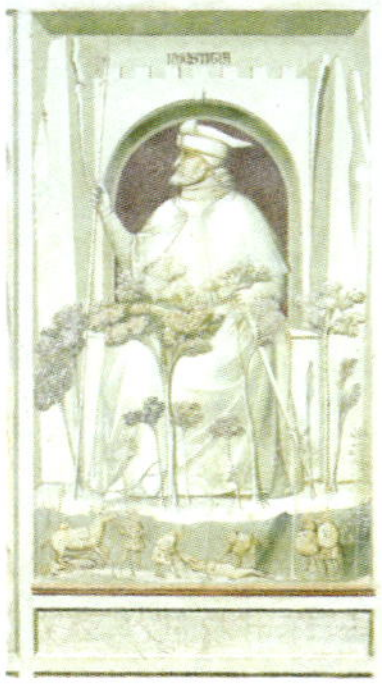

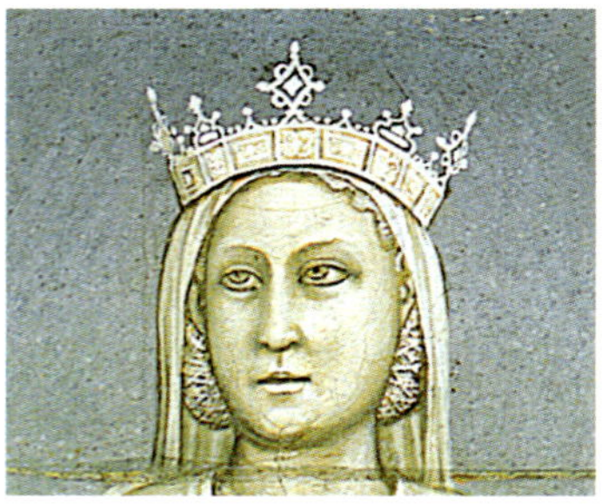

GIUSTIZIA

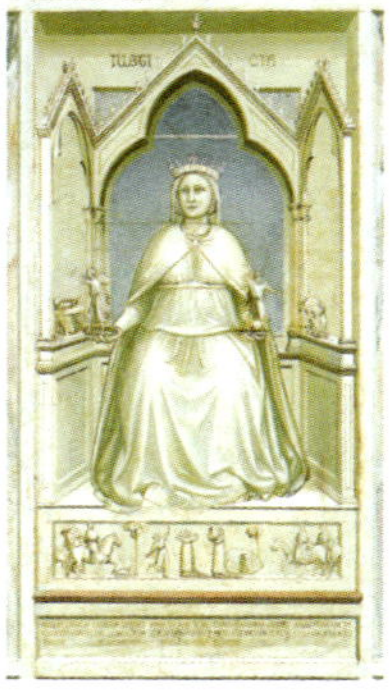

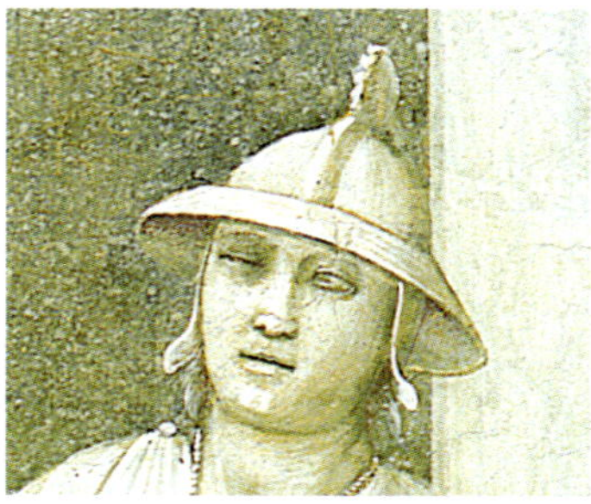

INFEDELTÀ

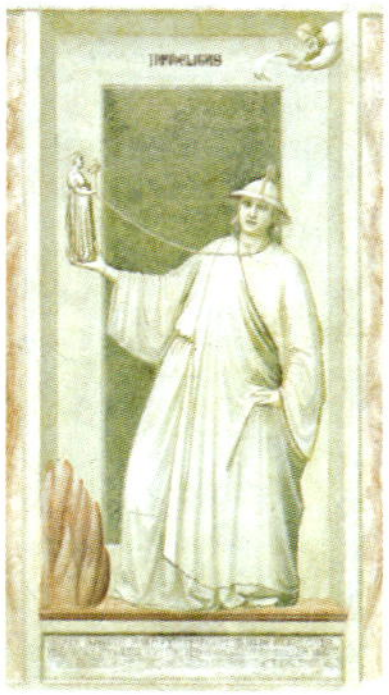

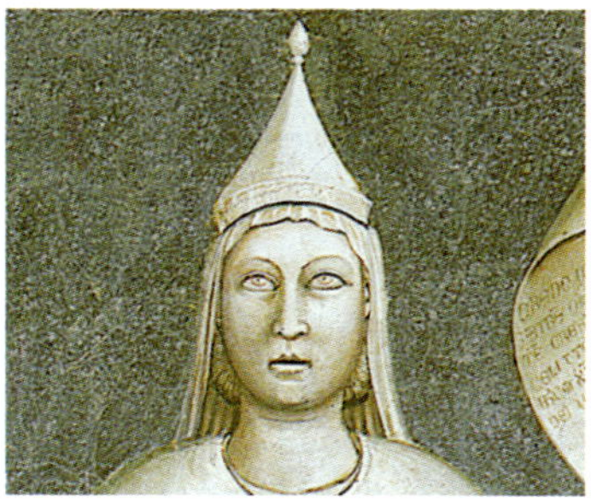

FEDE

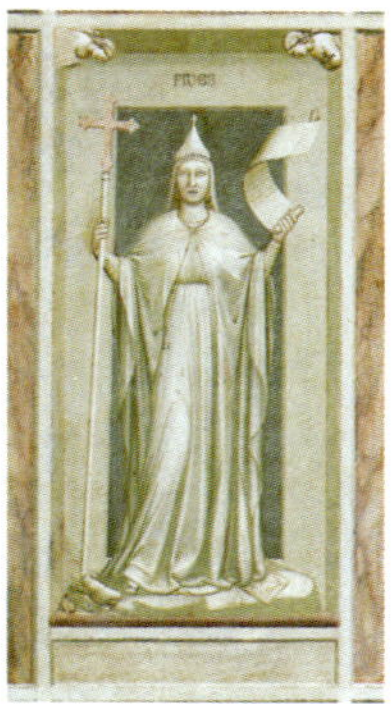

tion below. In her right hand she holds up a plate on which sits an angel crowning Good, while the angel held by the left hand is punishing Evil. On the dais at her feet, four horsemen — two hunters with dogs and a falcon, and two merchants — proceed confidently towards a village at feast time, where people are playing music and dancing.

Now we are right at the center of the Chapel. If we stand at a point equidistant between Justice and Injustice, and from here observe the three pairs of virtues and vices that precede and follow, we note that all are framed by little brackets that obliquely converge on this central point. Justice and Injustice are, instead, orthogonal with respect to the observer. They appear in deep perspective, and are completely by a dais illustrating their effects; finally, they are seated on a throne, in analogy both to Christ the Judge and Lucifer. As writes Dante in the Divine Comedy, with the aim to "take those who live in this life away from the state of misery and lead them to the state of happiness" ("Epistle to Cangrande") into the cradle of the universal empire and under the protection of St. Lucy, so Giotto paints so that — in the reign of justice, enemy of evil and, in particular, of usury — on this earth men can live "cum iocunditate". What clearly emerges is thus "the concept of earthly justice as a reflection of divine justice" (Basile).

V.A: INFIDELITAS: she limps because of a deformed left leg (thus reads the pedestal). She confides in the idol, held up with her right hand: that is, in the little statue that, in turn, fascinates her, offering her a blossoming bush with its right hand (the Epicurean-naturalistic horizon), while with her right hand she tightens a string ending in a hangman's knot, tied to the worshiper's neck. Choking, she will shortly fall into the red fires of Hell, dragged down by the idol which illudes her ("in-lude") and will soon delude her ("de-lude"). *Ludere*: to play with in order to fool. The idol appears as a representation of usury (Dante's wolf): the idol of the loan-shark.

V.B: FIDES: strong and self-confident, she looks you straight in the eye (like St. Peter in Pentecost, evoked, as well, by the key poking out of her cloak). With her left hand she holds up a scroll bearing the Nicene Creed; with her right, a cross mounted on a rod which is breaking the idol to pieces, there on the ground. Her feet trample on the tablets of astrological and cabalistic superstition. Schisms and heresies have opened painful tears in her cloak and tunic, but do not harm her face or body: nothing will make her limp.

VI.A: INVIDIA: this is the most diabolical and repugnant vice. Burnt by the fire at her feet, the fire of greed, she clasps in her left hand the purse containing her possessions, while the right hand reaches out greedily, somewhat like a clawed paw, or like the wide-open mouth of a poisonous snake. That diabolical snake then emerges from under her turban, comes out of her mouth and enters her eyes, poisoning her gaze. "In-vidia": a not-seeing, or a seeing of everything with an evil eye (while the enormous ear listens malignantly). "Patet hic invidiae cecae": this is the octosyllabic verse that we are able to read on the pedestal. Blind her, as in the mosaic

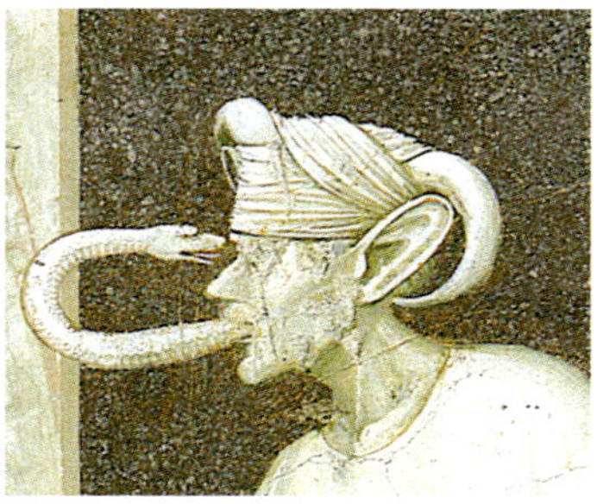

INVIDIA

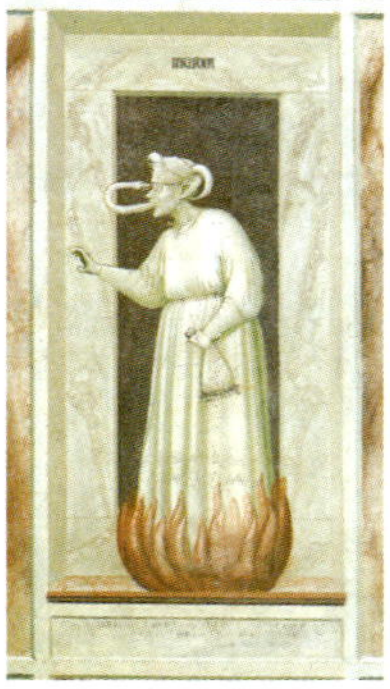

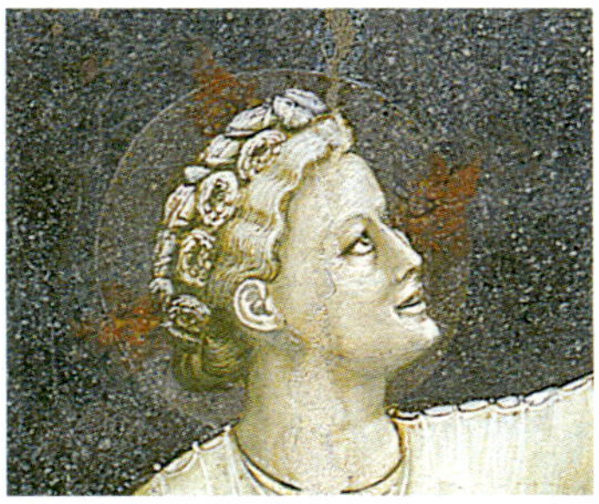

CARITÀ

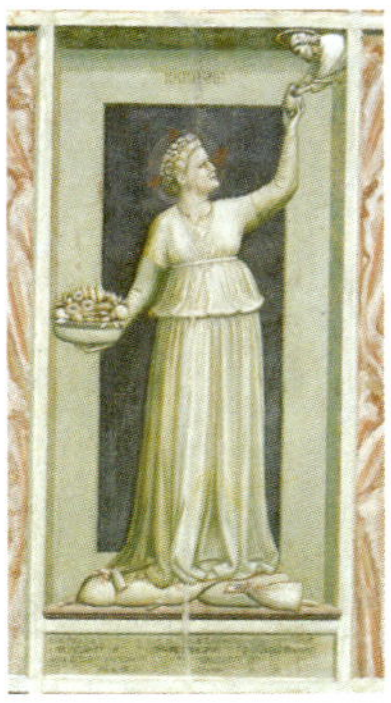

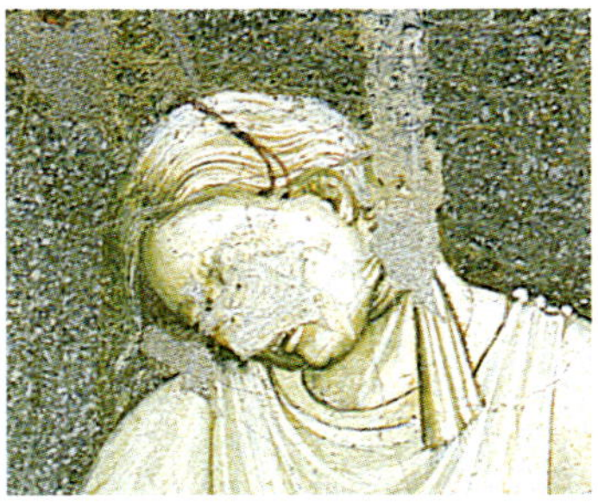

DISPERAZIONE

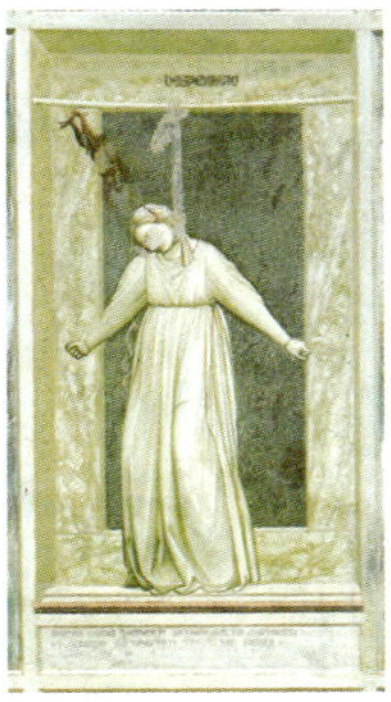

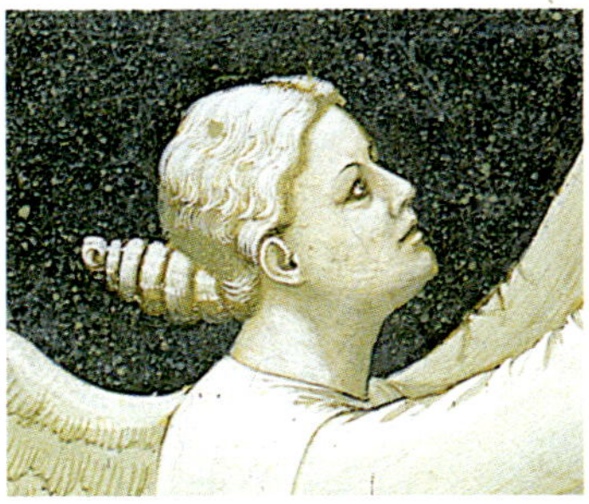

SPERANZA

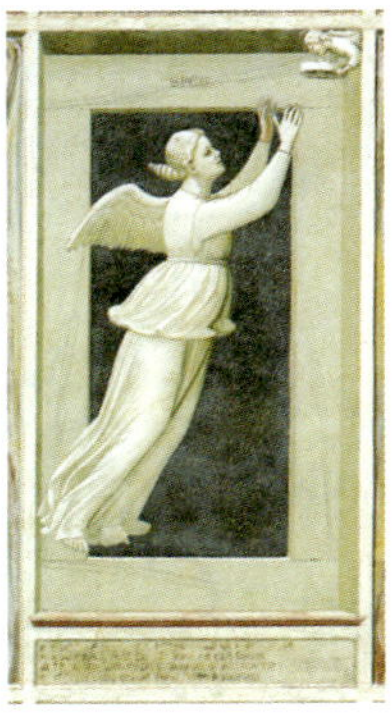

on the counter-façade at Torcello (where little snakes enter and leave the eye sockets; as in St. Thomas or in Dante's Purgatory, where all the envious have their eyelids pierced and sewn by wire (XIII, 70-71).

VI.B: KARITAS: her haloed head (with three red flashes of light evoking the halo of Christ) is crowned by flowers, her gaze turns intensely toward Jesus, to whom, with one hand, she offers her heart (and sees it given back to her), while with the other she offers her neighbor a basket full of flowers, fruit and ears of wheat: "Let your right hand not know what your left does". If invidia is "non-seeing", charity lies wholly in this gaze toward Destiny and in this acceptance of God's grace. Giving to one's neighbor, and trampling on the idol of possession (the purses full of money, perhaps gained by usury) come as a consequence.

VII.A: DESPERATIO: she hangs herself, just as the idol of *infidelitas* foreshadowed (and one's gaze flies toward Judas, right at the opposite end; and in the Judgment, choked to death). In the high right-hand corner, a sinister devil hooks her head, to drag her into the fires of hell, in the grand Final Judgment. Her face is devastated, her fists closed: the tragic end of deliberately-chosen evil.

VII.B: SPES: with calmed face, she takes flight, her hands reaching out toward the crown of glory, toward the Paradise of the Final Judgment. Her body, her head, her arms: each detail evokes the Christ of Ascension (note the wing of hope and the edge of Jesus' raised cloak).

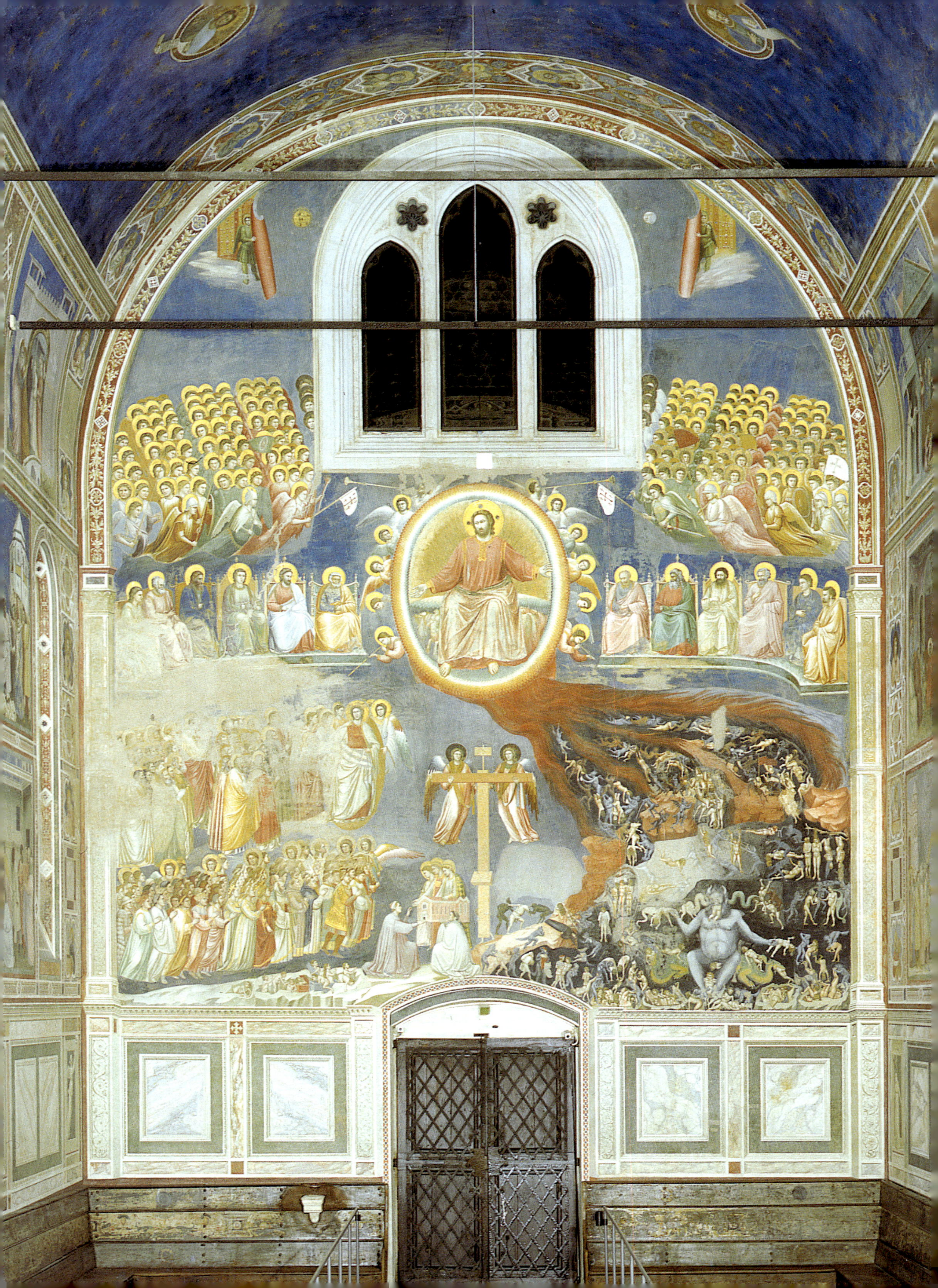

40. Final Judgment

All is clear and distinct. Our gaze is immediately, magnetically drawn to the focal center, the solar Christ the Judge, framed by the beam-encircled mandorla. The rainbow sent by God as a sign of the Ancient Covenant after the universal flood, reaches its symbolic apex in Christ, the New and Eternal Covenant. He, the Almighty, sits on the throne of jasper green below which we can make out the symbols of the four evangelists. Showing his glorious wounds, he comes to judge the world.

In him, everything is open toward the chosen, on his right: his gaze, his head, the wound on his side, his hand (while the other, the left hand, is closed over the reprobates of Hell). Seraphim encircle the mandorla. The judges flanking him are the twelve apostles, enthroned in a semicircle. On Christ's right are Peter, James, John, Philip, Simon and Thomas. On his left are Matthew, Andrew, Bartholomew, James the younger, Judas Thaddeus and Matthias. The three-mullioned window is not only a luminous opening from which the red vibration of hope enters at twilight; above all, it is a throne from which God, One-in-Three, descends and judges in the visible form of Christ. The two little flowers, each bearing six petals, which are incorporated in the cloverleaf or three-mullioned window, perfectly correspond to the two groups of six apostles who have descended with him. The eight other angelic choirs form a semicircle crowing the throne/three-mullioned window. On his left: angels, archangels, princes and potentates. On his right: virtues, dominations, thrones and cherubim. They seem to be placed in an orderly manner in the seats of a theater, in symmetrical rows structured along the pattern of the tercet (one more evocation of the Trinity). They are led by flagbearers. Michael and Gabriel, those nearest Christ the Judge, hold up the sword and banner of the Knights of the Holy Sepulcher, with its white crosses.

At the top of the grand fresco, two other angels are rolling up the thick carpet of heaven's vault (this is the end of the world!) against which stand out the golden sun and white moon; as if a reversible material had been woven: on the back of the human-blue (the sky as we see it from earth), shows the divine-red (which was foretasted at sunrise and sunset);and behind, appear — golden and gem-strewn — the gates of the eternal empyrean: "new heavens and new earth".

Behind Christ the judge as well, dressed in red and blue, gold shines forth. Giotto has not abolished the Byzantines' gold: except that, remembering St. Francis' Canticle of the Creatures, he has staged reality in its natural colors, for these bear the imprint of God's creating hand; these clothe the eternal Word; it is in their domain that the human game of liberty is played. "The event of the redemption is a 'human' story. The characters, even if their faces are transformed from the human by the stupendous beauty of 'Grace'," writes the fine critic, Bellinati, " set their feet solidly on earth, with its green, its flowers, its colors: earth intimately tied to the daily life of man". So — with his paintbrush, as did his near contemporary, Dante, with his pen — Giotto collaborated with popes and saints (Dominic and Thomas, Francis and Anthony...) in combating the spiritualism of the Catharist heresy (forerunner of today's New Age philosophy). The splendor of gold remains, but as ultimate Destiny.

From the mandorla pour forth the four fiery rivers of Hell, which drag into the abyss myriads of the damned, shoved down by leaden devils. The first river knocks down the usurers, marked by the white purse of dirty money tied to their neck. Choking money-lenders in life, eternally choked, in the Dantesque punishment of the contrapasso (Reginaldo Scrovegni, the usurer who was father to Enrico, appears in Canto XVII OF Dante's Inferno). Lowest of all, hanged and eviscerated, is Judas.

To the left of Christ the Judge stands Lucifer, enormous and sinister, modeled along the lines of the mosaic by Coppo di Marcovaldo which for around half a century had stood in the Baptistery of Florence. With human hands and ferociously clawed paws, he is tearing apart some souls; he devours three of them, with his human mouth and the two mouths of the "ancient snake" coming out of his ears. The horrid leviathan does the same — that Biblical dragon which symbolizes the power of this world, and serves Lucifer as a throne. All around is "eternal pain": indescribable suffering imposed on "people who are lost", attacked by devils. Giotto had his assistants paint many of these figures.

The chaos, the ugliness and disorder of Hell, is contrasted, to the right of Christ the Judge, by the three-part ascending crowd of the saved, in whose faces we perceive the unmistakable imprint of Giotto's hand: below, the little souls that — again covered by flesh — come our in surprise and adoration from the labyrinths of the earth; then the grand procession of the chosen, the clergy (bishops, priests, deacons, founders of religious orders ...) and people, men and women who have sanctified their lives by way of work and crafts (the fourth person on the left, wearing a white head covering, is perhaps Giotto's self-portrait); above, guided by Mary, the ancient saints of the Old Testament and the primitive Church.

At the foot of the cross kneels Enrico Scrovegni, wearing the purple habit of penance, and Altegrado de' Catanei — the erudite canonical priest of the cathedral, who collaborated with Giotto in structuring the work — offer the little model of the chapel to Mary, at whose sides stand St. John the Baptist and St. Catherine of Alexandria. The Madonna — who is represented more than twenty times in this Chapel dedicated to her — is the mediator between human fragility and merciful divine justice.

The last image that Giotto discreetly suggests to a careful observer, is a tiny detail: at the foot of the grand cross (and almost as if to give it legs, so that it can move toward man) is a little human figure. He participates in exalting the cross: two great angels hold him up, and he — we can see his feet, and glimpse his head — clasps to his heart the *dulce lignum*. A fragile little man — a good thief, the man from Cyrene, each of us — who has come across that Man, has recognized him as God, and has grown fond of him: he thus bears "the sweet yoke, the light burden", in the high prospect of happiness, whose earnest is — here and now — the joy of a future "hundredfold".

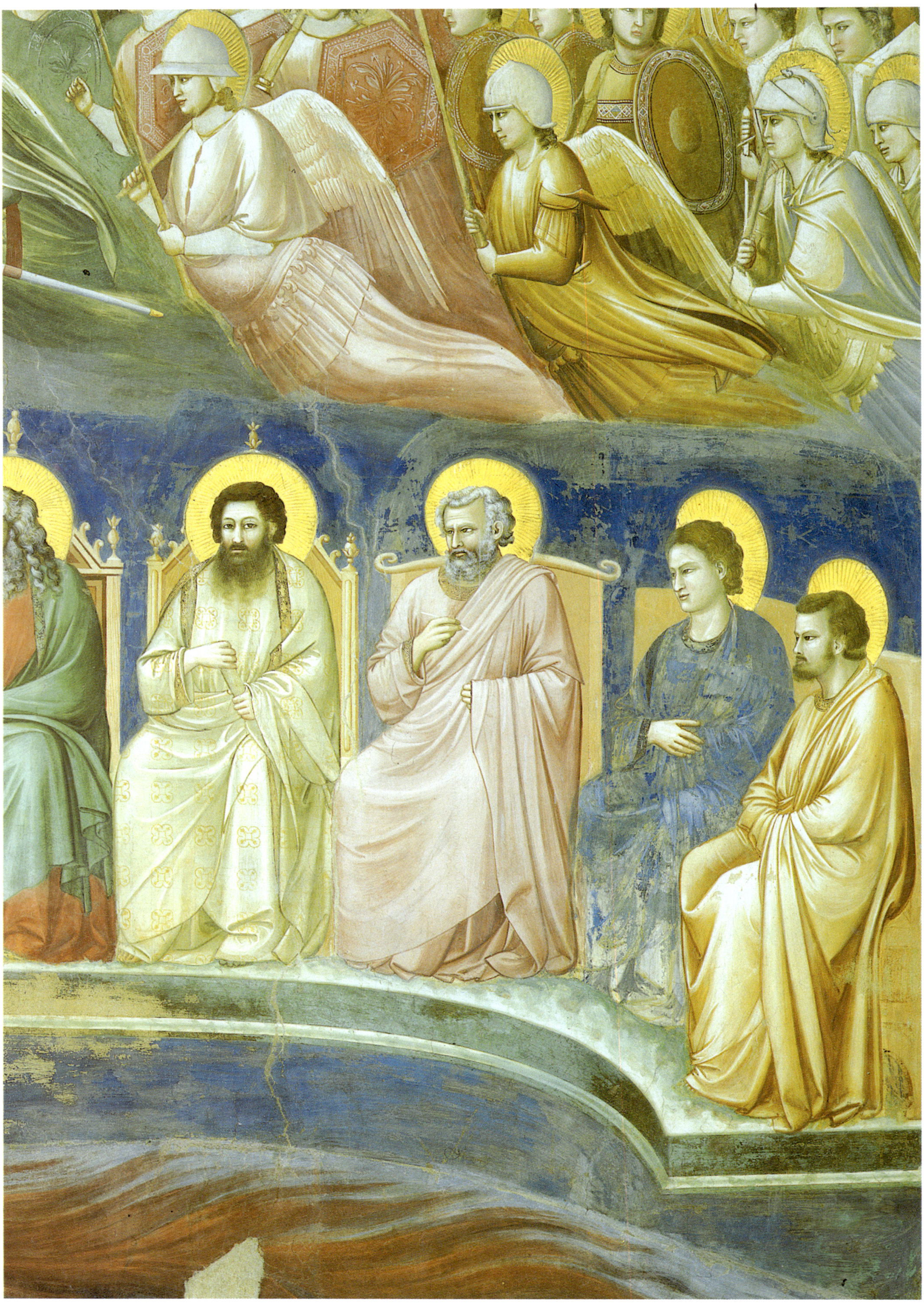